BELLAMY, J.
Cornwall - a look back

1898343071

CORNWALL COUNTY COUNCIL
LIBRARY SERVICES

ONE AND ALL

Cornwall –
A Look Back

A scrapbook of memories

by
Jean Bellamy

Newmill Books
St Austell

First published in 2002 by
Newmill Books
an imprint of DGR Books
Kenwyn
Greensplat
St Austell, Cornwall PL26 8XX
England

ISBN 1 898343 07 1

BY THE SAME AUTHOR

Children's fiction
Cornish Mystery (1986)
The Haunted Island (1990)
The Tomb of the Black Gull (1997)

Also:
Treasures of Dorset (1991)
Dorset Quiz Book (1995)
A Second Dorset Quiz Book (1997)
The Dorset Tea Trail (1999)

CONTENTS

ACKNOWLEDGEMENTS

Vicar of Morwenstow and *Cornish Characters and Strange Events* (1913)
    by S. Baring-Gould
The Story of An Ancient Parish (1913) by H. R. Coulthard
The Story of Cornwall (1934) by A. K. Hamilton Jenkin
The semi-precious stones of Cornwall by G. F. Leechman
History of Cornwall by Fortescue Hitchins

DEDICATION

*I dedicate this book to the memory of my father, who had been a visitor to Cornwall
from his youth – and to that of my mother, who came to love the county too.*

FOREWORD

At the south-westernmost tip of the British Isles, the rugged granite outcrop that is Cornwall projects itself into the Atlantic. Almost an island, it possesses the longest coastline of any county in the country, and visitors in days gone by were regarded with suspicion by the natives, who looked upon all folk from over the border as 'furreigners'.

For the visitor crossing the Tamar, there was always that strange, all-pervasive sense of having entered upon another land. As someone once said, "When I cross back into England, I feel like presenting my passport!" Today much has altered, and in the name of progress, one speeds westwards along the A30 which – spinelike and intrusive, though convenient – divides the county into two. Car-parks and petrol stations have inevitably sprouted, and crowds throng many of the beaches.

Yet the sense of 'difference' still lingers, for there is much that has not, and cannot, change. Today, Cornwall, though invaded by the motor-car, subjected to commercialisation and all that that involves, and descended upon by hordes of visitors and sightseers during the summer months, nevertheless still generates its own indefinable aura of mystery and charm.

Much has already been written about Cornwall, but in the following pages I have tried to recapture something of the magic of Cornwall past. More specifically, I have endeavoured to recall, by means of photographs and childhood memories, the Cornwall of the 1930s and what it meant to me – as well as to many other folk, I suspect, who spent their pre-war holidays in the land of the Tre, Pol and Pen.

Jean Bellamy

I love to be beside the sea on sunny summer days
Upon the golden sands to rest, to feel the sun's warm rays,
To hear the water lap the shore with peaceful murmuring sound
And watch the tide flow gently in o'er pebbles smooth and round.

I love to clamber over rocks, in little pools to peep,
To scramble up the rough cliff paths and rocky steps so steep,
To wander on the lonely cliffs and see, far, far below
Some tiny cove with smooth white sand where footsteps rarely go.

I love to climb the rough stone walls, to hear the cattle low,
To tread upon the springy turf, where tufts of sea-pink grow;
To watch the woolly frightened sheep, to hear the hum of bees,
To view the fields where golden corn sways gently in the breeze.

I love to see the rugged coast sweep far from east to west,
To watch a gull with mournful screech sink gracefully to rest,
To gaze upon the tranquil sea of deepest sapphire blue,
To watch a tiny sailing boat drift gently into view.

And when the summer days are gone and autumn winds blow chill,
When visitors have all gone home, I love the seaside still,
To go down to the lonely sands and feel the salty spray,
To watch the clouds go scudding by in skies of leaden grey.

And when the great Atlantic waves go thundering up the shore
To pound against the granite cliffs with mighty echoing roar,
I turn to where the fishing boats safe in the harbour lie,
And hear above the howling wind the curlew's plaintive cry.

And when the evening shadows fall and fishermen set sail,
Often perhaps their lives to risk mid tempest storm and gale,
I pray that they may be preserved from perils of the night,
And safe into the harbour come, with the return of light.

J.E.B.

Down Memory Lane

Gigantic cliffs and tossing seas, golden sands and rocky outcrops; tiny coves, picturesque harbours; fishing boats at anchor, fishermen mending their nets against the harbour wall; the smell of tar and the salt sea-air; the screech of gulls.

Narrow twisting lanes and profusions of wild flowers; disused tin-mines standing starkly beautiful against the skyline, their ruined engine-houses alongside.

Surfing in rough seas, battling with huge breakers; scrambling over rock-strewn beaches; fishing in tiny rock-pools.

Crab and lobster salad, great bowls of Cornish cream. (6d. was the price my father paid for a cream tea when he first went down to Cornwall.)

Days out by charabanc – packed lunches with delicious meat-filled Cornish pasties; brilliant seas and clear light; grey granite villages; Cornish piskie brooches on sale in little gift shops.

The harmonious singing of Cornish choirs.

These are amongst my memories of the Cornwall of yesteryear.

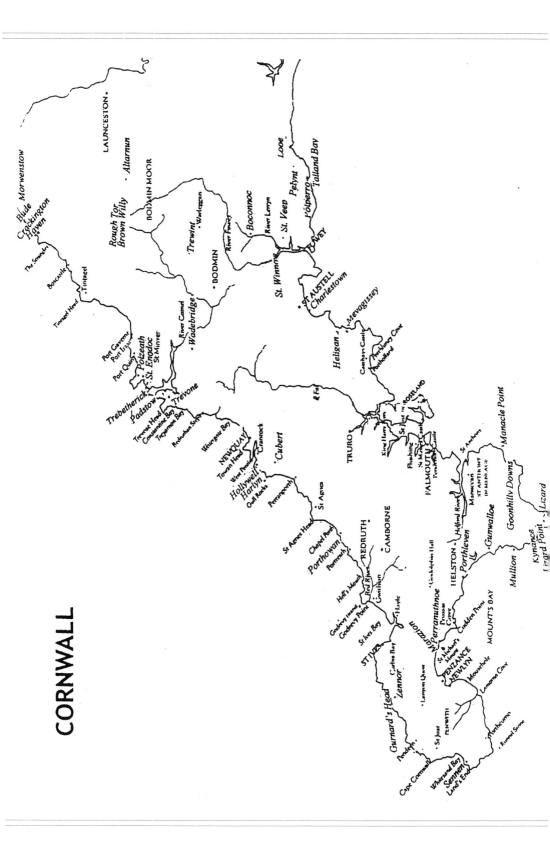

NORTH CORNWALL

1.
MORWENSTOW

On a hillside in a place of extreme stillness and seclusion stands a venerable old church, its grey stone tower silhouetted against the blue of the Atlantic, its churchyard terminating at the edge of the sheer cliff-face.

This is the tiny, remote parish of Morwenstow, near Bude, famous for its eccentric parson, the Reverend Robert Stephen Hawker, who ministered here for forty-one years, from 1834 until his death in 1875. He is believed to have been responsible for instituting the service of Harvest Festival in the Church of England. For early in his incumbency he addressed a notice to his parishioners, calling on them to assemble at the church for the purpose of giving thanks for the harvest.

A grandson of the well-known Dr Hawker, incumbent of Charles Church in Plymouth, Hawker was born on the 3rd December 1804 at Stoke Damarel in Devon. He grew up a mischievous, high-spirited boy, much given to practical joking – a propensity which continued on into adult life. His father, a poor curate, was unable to maintain him at Oxford, so Hawker hit upon a way out of the dilemma. At Efford, near Bude, lived four sisters, each of whom had been left an annuity of £200, as well as lands and a fine house. Hawker saw this as his opportunity, and without waiting to put on his hat, he ran from Stratton to Bude. Arriving "hot and blown", he proposed to Miss Charlotte who, at forty-one, was a year older than his mother. She accepted him and they seem to have lived happily until her death in 1863.

It was while at Oxford that Hawker scared the wits out of the superstitious inhabitants of Bude by perpetrating the prank for which he has become famous. At full moon in July 1825, he swam out to a rock and plaited seaweed into a wig which he placed on his head so that it hung around him in lank streamers. With his legs enveloped in oilskins, flashing moonbeams about from a hand-mirror, he sang, screamed, and wailed disconsolately; until, having attracted the attention of passers-by, he dived off the rock and disappeared, returning the next night and repeating the performance.

Crowds assembled each evening to look for the mermaid braiding her tresses out at sea, the strange pantomime continuing for several nights. Mystified folk began to arrive from nearby Stratton, Kilkhampton and all the villages round about, and with telescopes trained upon the rock, listened bewildered to the weird sounds emanating therefrom. Eventually, hoarse, cold and tired, Hawker wound up the performance by singing the National Anthem, then plunged into the waves and disappeared, after which the 'mermaid' was not seen again.

As a curate, Hawker owned a black pig called Gyp, "well cared for, washed and curry-combed", which ran beside him when he went walking and visiting. It even entered ladies' drawing-rooms, sometimes to their displeasure – at which he would order his pet forth and it would leave the room with its tail "out of curl".

Another amusing tale concerns Hawker's dislike of dissenters. Walking on the cliffs near Morwenstow one day with a parson friend, a gust of wind carried the latter's hat over the edge of the cliff. A week or two later, a Methodist preacher at Truro was discoursing on the efficacy of prayer and related an incident that had occurred when he was on his way to Bude. He was wearing a "shocking bad hat" and blushed to think of entering the watering-place so ill adorned. So he prayed, then looked up to heaven and saw a black spot coming down. As it largened and widened, he found it to be a brand-new hat by a distinguished London maker. Throwing his old beaver into the sea he went on to Bude wearing the new hat.

"The rascal made off with Vincent's new hat from Bennett's!" proclaimed the Vicar of Morwenstow, incensed. "There was no reaching him, for we were on the cliff and could not descend the precipice. He was deaf enough, I promise you, to our shouts!"

Soon after his induction to Morwenstow, Hawker abandoned his cassock – in which he found it difficult to scramble about the cliffs – for a claret-coloured coat with long tails. He disliked anything black, the only black he would wear being his boots. Beneath the claret coat which he wore open, was displayed a knitted blue fisherman's jersey with a little red cross woven into it, and fishing-boots reaching above the knee completed the outfit. The claret cassock coats, when worn out, were passed on to the maidservants.

Outside Morwenstow Church

He also took to wearing a strange yellow garment about the house and around the parish, which he acquired as the result of a conversation with a neighbour. On complaining to the latter that he could not get a greatcoat to suit his fancy, the neighbour suggested that he wear a poncho.

"What is that?" enquired the vicar.

"Nothing but a blanket with a hole in the middle," came the reply.

"Do you put your legs through the hole, and tie the four corners over your head?"

"No!" said the neighbour and fetched one for the vicar to try on. The garment pleased Hawker tremendously and on his next visit to Bideford he bought a yellowish-brown blanket and cut a hole in the middle through which he put his head.

After living for the first few years at Morwenstow in a rented house, Hawker built the vicarage with chimneys resembling the towers of churches with which he had had connections – Tamerton, Magdalen Hall, Welcombe in North Devon, and Morwenstow. When in need of inspiration, he would escape to a little hut which he had made himself, set on the side of the cliff below the church. If you look, you may still see it there, its sides formed of the curved ribs of boats, its entrance ornamented with carvings from a figurehead. Here Hawker would sit, sheltered from the storm, looking out across the churning ocean, composing poetry or watching ships scudding dangerously near the cliff in the teeth of the gale.

When his wife died on 2nd February 1863 (she was by that time an elderly lady and blind) Hawker fell into a deep depression, moping about the cliffs or in his study and losing interest in everything. He did not remain long in this state, however, for in December 1864 he remarried. This time it was to someone much younger than himself – a Polish young lady of twenty-three by whom he had three children.

In 1875 his health began to deteriorate, and he died at Plymouth, whence he and his wife had travelled, probably to seek medical advice. His funeral took place there on Wednesday, 18th August 1875, in the Roman Catholic Cathedral, following which there was considerable controversy surrounding his apparent death-bed conversion to the Roman Catholic faith. There was great sadness, too, that he had not been interred at his beloved Morwenstow; for it had long been his wish that he should be buried beside his wife inside the church, a space having been left in the stone for his name to be added.

Morwenstow people are said to have seen the old man standing at the head of the stone looking mournfully at the blank space.

2.
BUDE

The golden beaches of Cornwall's rugged north coast – amongst them Bude, Polzeath, Newquay and Perranporth, have attracted surf-bathers in their thousands over the years. Not in the style of the surf-riders of today, with their wet-suits and spectacular acrobatics, but using the less adventurous surf-board – or 'body-boards' as they are now termed.

Looking back to pre-war days, attitudes seemed a little more relaxed where bathing was concerned, though one was always aware of the dangers and careful not to take risks. There was that familiar figure, the man with the megaphone, shouting warnings to over-adventurous surfers (as he still does), and red flags which warned bathers that it is unsafe to enter the water at certain parts of the beach or times of the tide – as they still do. Life-saving equipment is probably more sophisticated today, though it was always on hand on the more dangerous beaches. Bude and Perranporth in particular are remembered as being hazardous at low-water due to the numerous pot-holes left by the receding tide.

Surfing in the sea off Crooklets Beach, however, or enjoying the salt-water swimming pool on Summerleaze Beach, were highlights of our pre-war holiday in Bude. Apart from being rather more populated during the season nowadays, the town appears much as it always was. The Sir Thomas Ackland Bathing Pool, tucked away amongst the rocks on the eastern side of Summerleaze, seems to be little used nowadays.

Well-remembered was our visit to the rambling old rectory at Bude where the elderly incumbent related a strange story. Laid up during an illness, he dreamed one night of a hooded figure standing at the foot of his bed. Told by his nocturnal visitor to get up and follow him, he obeyed and was led by the monk to a secret chapel within the rectory. On recovering from his illness, the rector recalled his dream and, remembering where the monk had led him, looked for the chapel and found it.

Sir Thomas Bathing Pit, Bude, *c*. 1907.

Born in the manor house at nearby Stratton in the early 1600s was one, Anthony Payne, the son of a tenant farmer. The registers do not go far enough back to record his actual date of birth, but so vast was his size that at school other pupils would work out their arithmetic lessons in chalk on his back. Sometimes they would even draw a map of the world, and he would return home like Atlas, carrying it on his shoulders. At the age of twenty-one, he measured seven feet two inches and thereafter grew two inches higher. However, he was not tall and lanky but stout and well proportioned. On one occasion he carried a bacon-hog from Kilkhampton to Stowe where he had gone to work, and during the Civil War (Cornwall was for the King), he drilled and manoeuvred the recruits from Kilkhampton and Stratton. He died, aged almost eighty, on 13th July 1691.

3.
CRACKINGTON HAVEN

Notable amongst my memories of this village just down the coast from Bude is the steepness of the descent from our guest house at the top of the hill to the cove, not to mention the ascent later in the day. It was one in five, or as they say today, 20%.

One usually caught the bus on the return journey, the younger passengers, I well remember, being requested to alight half-way up the hill to lighten the load.

The photograph of the water-splash shows a surprising number of cars in the car-park.

Splash and car park, Crackington Haven, 1936.

4.
TINTAGEL

Memories of this village include clambering down the steep, rocky descent for a swim in the delightful little sandy cove known as Bossiney with its Elephant Rock. Also, braving the even steeper descent to Benoath, the long sandy beach adjacent, where one afternoon the rain descended without warning. Hastily gathering up our picnic-tea and swimming gear, we made tracks for the long, now slippery, trek up the cliff path. Expecting to be half-drowned by the time we arrived back at our guest house 'Hollydene', how grateful we were to be met half-way up by Mr Irons, its owner. Thoughtfully, he had brought along our macs and umbrellas, thus saving us a severe soaking.

Another memory was visiting nearby Boscastle, approached by a steep hill and a sharp hairpin bend; also the delights of a surf bathe at lovely Trebarwith, which two places are little altered. Perhaps the same cannot be said of Tintagel which has become rather commercialised of late, though it still has charm.

Elephant Rock, Bossiney.

A remarkable inhabitant of the village in days gone by was one, Charles Chilcott, (next in size to Anthony Payne of Stratton [see *Bude*, p.14]), who died on 5th April 1815 in his sixtieth year. Six feet four inches in height and six feet nine inches around the chest, he weighed 460 pounds (nearly thirty-three stone). He smoked a two-inch-long pipe, and got through three pounds of tobacco a week. One of his stockings would have accommodated six gallons of wheat.

5.
AN ANCIENT CUSTOM

One of Cornwall's best-known and most popular customs is connected with the celebration of the coming of spring and the resurgence of new life after the long, dreary days of winter. The Celts believed that at this time of the year, when the leaves returned to the trees, the flowers bloomed, and the birds sang again, Gwydian, the god of vegetation, was reborn. They marked this occasion with great rejoicing and festivity.

So came into being the Helston Furry, or Floral, Dance, as it came to be known, celebrated from earliest times right down to the present day. The great occasion takes place, as everyone knows, on May 8th, when the little Cornish market town is decorated with flags and bunting and the locals don their glad rags and let their hair down. Fun and frivolity are the order of the day as they dance up and down the street, in through the front door and out by the back of every house, while the local band churns out the haunting, if somewhat monotonous refrain of the 'Cornish Floral Dance'.

Later in the season, other Cornish towns and villages repeat the occasion for the benefit of the holidaymakers; and to participate for the first time in such an age-old tradition on a balmy summer's evening is quite an experience. The village in question is Port Isaac and the scene will, no doubt, be familiar to many.

* * * * *

Dusk is falling over the village and there is magic in the air as we descend to the harbour by way of a narrow footpath between irregular white-washed cottages. The local band is assembled on the harbour plat where the entire village seems to have gathered. Residents rub shoulders with visitors and gnarled fishermen lean on the sea-wall, smoking their pipes. Gulls stand around squawking and squabbling over fish, and out to sea fishing boats rock gently at anchor.

Floral Dance.

We take up our position by a pile of lobster-pots, and as the band rolls out one old familiar tune after another, our feet tap out the rhythm on the cobbled paving-stones. Suddenly the music stops and there is a pause before the band strikes up again, this time with the catchy, repetitive melody of the Cornish Floral Dance. A dozen or so youngsters – the experts – step forward to lead the way in groups of four; then others, young and not so young, tag on behind and the procession grows.

After a discreet practice in a corner, we feel brave enough to join in, and off we go, hand in hand, two by two, to the accompaniment of the oft-repeated refrain which contains only nineteen notes. A few steps forward, exchanging partners, joining hands, circling, linking hands again, with ever increasing confidence we follow on up the hill, the band blowing indefatigably to the rear. Cameras click on all sides, capturing the romance of the summer evening; the laughter of the dancers mingles with that of the onlookers. Arriving hot and dishevelled at the top, we sit down on the grass to recover our breath while the bandsmen pause to get their second wind.

Then away we go again, tripping light-heartedly downhill in the gathering dusk, spurred on by the cheers of the spectators. As the tempo of the music quickens, faster and faster goes the procession, a whirling bobbing mass of humanity. Hopelessly entangled by now, we stumble back, tired but happy, to the harbour plat as the last notes of the music die away.

Distant lights twinkle across the silent sea as the dancers disperse into the night. As we set off up the tortuous path between the slumbering cottages, all is still save for the lap of the tide against the harbour wall. It has been an unforgettable evening of Cornish enchantment.

✳ ✳ ✳ ✳ ✳

(Up to the last century, Port Isaac was known as 'Portissick' – 'Port' = Beach; 'Issick' = Cornfield.)

Harbour, Port Isaac.

6.
A DESERTED VILLAGE

Most visitors to Port Quin these days are probably unaware of the tragedy that occurred in this little hamlet around the turn of the century. Situated between Polzeath and Port Isaac, it comprises a small cove with a handful of cottages. Yet, until disaster struck one night, it must have been the centre of quite a flourishing fishing industry, to judge by the size of its pilchard palace.

The tragic drama which rendered Port Quin silent and deserted occurred about the year 1900, and it was probably around two years later that my father visited the village. Struck by the uncanny silence and general air of desolation that overhung the little place, he learnt how the fishing fleet set sail one night, never to return. The next day, with the male population, small though it was, wiped out at one stroke, the stricken widows and their families packed up their few belongings and departed, leaving their cottages and all that was in them.

In recent years I have heard it said that this version of events was an exaggeration – even a legend! However, this is as it was told to my father by a local fisherman *c.* 1900, and most Cornish folk, I am told, believe the story to be true.

For years Port Quin remained silent and abandoned. Visiting it for the first time in the 1960s, we found it still uninhabited and overhung by an almost tangible gloom. We climbed the steep hill on the west side, passing crumbling cottages overgrown with bushes and shrubs, bearing witness to the events of sixty years previously.

A return visit about twenty years later, however, revealed a transformation, for on that hot August afternoon, holidaymakers basked on the beach, and on the low cliff above, cottages stood restored, refurbished and available for summer lettings. The National Trust had taken over the surrounding area and Port Quin appeared no different from any

Port Quin, 1983.

other Cornish cove. Only the ruins of the derelict cottages on the hill, even more desolate and overgrown, were a reminder of Port Quin's sad past.

The only building of any size in the village is the one used in olden times as a 'pilchard palace'. This building is a relic of bygone days when the fishing industry of Cornwall took place on a much larger scale than it does today. Pilchards were caught in a great sheet of mesh, made mostly at Bridport in Dorset, with cork floats lying along one edge and leaded weights along the other. At the beginning of the season, the huge fishing fleet would be taken down to the water laden with children singing traditional songs. The children would disembark and the fishermen would go aboard and take up their positions in the bay. On the headland the look-out man, or 'huer', would keep watch from his hut. (Huer huts are today popular tourist haunts). As soon as a reddish-brown or purple stain on the sea told the huer that a shoal had arrived, he would sound a blast on his tin trumpet and the watchers on the shore would shout "Hevva, hevva!" (Cornish for 'shoal'). At which all the women would turn out of their houses and join the children on the beach.

The boats having been manoeuvred into position, the nets (or seines) would be let out in such a way as to trap millions of fish. These were then drawn into the shallow water by tow ropes attached to capstans on shore, from whence they were scooped into the boats with baskets, and conveyed away to the pilchard palaces (or cellars) in carts. Once there, the children would hand the fish to the women, who stacked them in rows, a layer of salt being placed above each row until the stack was roof-high. Often they worked all night on the 'balking', as it was called, or even several nights on end, helpers coming from adjacent villages to lend a hand. The fish would be left piled up in this way for about a month, after which they would be washed and put into barrels, each containing 2,000, by fish maidens. After being pressed for nine or ten days, most of the catch was exported, though some of it would be sold fresh in the surrounding areas.

The four main ports in the nineteenth century were Fowey, Falmouth, St Ives and Penzance. Many types of fish were caught, though by far the most important was the pilchard which would appear in huge shoals off the coast. The season usually lasted from July to October or sometimes later, and the number of pilchards sent off from these ports would have been around ninety million a year.

During the twentieth century, however, the industry dwindled and by the 1930s was beginning to disappear. Today, though not entirely gone, it is very small and the fish are caught far out at sea by drift-net, in the same way as mackerel and herring. Several reasons have been given for the decline of the industry, but it is generally believed to have been brought about by the increase in deep-sea trawling which causes the break up of shoals and the destruction of many young fish.

7.
A BURIED CHURCH

Returning to a place after a lapse of years is always a nostalgic experience, and revisiting the ancient church of St Enodoc at Trebetherick, close to the river Camel near Padstow was no exception. The little church stands surrounded by a golf course and is included, along with the chapelry of St Michael at Porthilly, Rock, in the parish of St Minver (Sancta Menefreda). All three churches are bounded by the Atlantic and the Camel Estuary on three sides, the eastern boundary running north and south from Port Quin to Trewornan Bridge. At one time, St Enodoc was almost completely covered by sand, until dug out and restored in 1864.

Approaching across the green sward (and being careful to avoid the golf balls), the first thing one notices is a crooked spire with its tip missing sticking up above rising ground. I learned of the legend connected with the spire back in the 1930s, though locals to whom I spoke on a more recent visit seemed, rather surprisingly, not to have heard of it. According to the story told us by the vicar of the time, a passing donkey nibbled off the tip of the spire when the church lay buried – and who knows but what the legend was not true.

The south aisle of the little building was built in the fifteenth century to replace the original Norman south transept. At this time too, a finely-carved screen was added, separating the nave from the chancel. Of this, however, all that remains is the present screen, the upper part having been removed, rather clumsily, during the eighteenth and nineteenth centuries when the chapel lay buried. The locals at that time took to calling St Enodoc 'Siskininny Church', being probably under the impression that the building was sinking.

The only means of entry into the church was through the roof, which had begun to fall into disrepair. It is not known how often the building was used, but it is said that at least once a year the vicar let

St Enodoc Church.

himself into the north transept by this means in order to conduct a service – this being necessary in order to comply with ecclesiastical law. The year of the last recorded marriage was 1851, though a wedding did take place as recently as 1955 after a service at the parish church, St Enodoc being no longer licensed for marriages.

In a first-hand account dated 1919-21, lent to a recent incumbent and written by the Rev. Hart Smith, it was reported that "sands had blown higher than the eastern gable, the wet coming in freely. The high pews were mouldy-green and worm-eaten, there were bats living in the belfry, and the Communion Table had two short legs because the rock projected at the foot of the east wall."

The restoration of the church makes interesting reading. The walls were partially rebuilt on good foundations, the sand was removed, and new seats provided. The little churchyard was cleared and fenced with a good wall. It all cost about £650, and much effort went into raising the money. Nothing was destroyed unnecessarily or taken away if it was of use or interest, and a great deal of loving care went into the work which was carried out by the masons and workmen of the parish.

Of the tombs in the churchyard, the oldest one dates from the fifteenth century, traces of earlier tombs having been lost at the time of the restoration. By the western boundary wall is to be found the grave of Sir John Betjeman's mother, her husband being commemorated by an oval plaque inside the church – a fact which had particular relevance on the day we visited in 1984. For Sir John Betjeman, the Poet Laureate from 1972, had just died, and to the right of the churchyard was a freshly-dug grave marked by an assortment of faded flowers and a sprinkling of cards carrying four-lined poems.

The grave of Sir John Betjeman.

The view looking across the golf course to nearby Daymer Bay was considered by Betjeman to be the finest sight in Cornwall. Going back into the dim, distant past, it is known that in prehistoric times the intervening sand-dunes (between church and sea) were a dense forest inhabited by wild animals. In 1857 a great gale shifted the sand, leaving exposed twelve feet below high-tide mark, the roots and stumps of oaks, hazel-nut trees and yews, along with the teeth and horns of deer and other animals. Also found here were the remains of a village, with furniture still inside the houses – vacated, it is believed, in haste when the village, like the church, became engulfed during a sand-storm. In later years the whole area became covered over once more.

Tearing ouselves away from this fascinating spot, for time was going on, we thought back to a previous visit. On that occasion, having crossed the golf course to the beach for a quick dip in the sea (or more correctly, the Camel Estuary), we had dressed hastily and snatched up our belongings when the tide started flowing in. With other holidaymakers, also intent on beating the tide, we paddled round the base of the cliff, the rapidly rising water rippling around our knees. We made it, however, and landed safely on the sands of Daymer Bay, saved the necessity of retracing our steps by the longer route across the golf links. We had been in no danger and the race against the tide had been exhilarating.

8.
CORNISH ORIGINS

From where did the Cornish originate? A small dark race, they are believed by some to have descended from soldiers and sailors rescued from the wrecked battleships of the Spanish Armada. Another version is that at the dawn of history, Cornwall – like the whole of England – was inhabited by a race, also small and dark, who came to be known as the Ivernians. Today they survive not only along the coastline of western Cornwall, but also in south Wales.

At one time, the Ivernian race were said to have covered much of Cornwall, for numerous chippings from the manufacture of their first implements have been found in many parts of the county. They used sharpened flint fragments as knives and axes and for a long period they existed under Stone Age conditions. Later came the Celts to this country, who were divided into two distinct branches – the Brythons and the Goidels. The Brythons, who were culturally superior, slaughtered the Goidels and drove them into the remote corners of north and west Britain. Later, the Brythons were in turn driven out by the Saxons.

As the Celts of both branches advanced, they made slaves of the Ivernians, who retreated to the extreme westerly parts of the county and took refuge in caves along the coastline. Probably both Celts and Ivernians would practise a primitive type of nature worship: as, for instance, the great Festival of Springtime, at which season they celebrated the rebirth of Gwydian (or Gwythian), the god of vegetation, whose death occurred with the withering of the leaves in autumn, and the ingathering of the harvest.

Thus came into being the folk customs and ceremonies which once played a major part in the life of many towns and villages up and down this country, these festivities marking the passage of the seasons as the years went by. Nowadays this aspect of rural life has largely disappeared, though in a few places these fascinating ancient customs still survive.

9.
THE HOBBY-HORSE

For me, the little fishing port of Padstow is for ever linked with the gyrations of the Hobby-Horse, for to the very young the sight can be somewhat alarming. Dancing and prancing his way around the circle of onlookers, bumping and threatening the crowd, he presented quite a fearsome spectacle.

It was August and this display had been put on for the benefit of the holidaymakers; for the Hobby-Horse is normally a May Day celebration and one which used to be considered very important to the Cornish in the far-distant past. It is thought to have been an ancient fertility rite, a fact probably forgotten by generations of Padstow revellers down the centuries. One writer, however, was not enamoured of the custom, referring to it as "a very rough and coarse pastime" and "a relic of barbarianism".

It would appear to have been a custom not confined to Cornwall

Padstow, 1938.

either; for Scott in 'The Abbot' states, "...one fellow with a horse's head – painted – before him, and a tail behind, the whole covered with a long footcloth which was supposed to hide the body of the animal, ambled, carolled, pranced and plunged as he performed the celebrated part of the Hobby-Horse."

The Padstow version, involving a tall black, white and red head-gear tapering to a tuft of horsehair, appears to have been even more gruesome. The festivities would start at midnight from an inn in the town, and in front of the Hobby-Horse would dance a man in a mask, bedecked with flowers and carrying a brightly-coloured club with which to tease the horse. As to the carolling, this would have been performed by singers in the audience – not by the man beneath the stifling weight of the horse. For he would have had little breath left for singing as he gyrated non-stop throughout the day.

Except, that is, for the moments when the musician's song faded away to a pianissimo, the club came to rest, and horse and dancer sank to the ground. Then suddenly the music would liven up and the horse would return to life again, the dancer continuing his dancing and teasing of the horse, the crowds surging on through the streets, or gathering around the maypole.

The custom still takes place today, of course, though in a modified form. On May Day each year as of old, the Hobby-Horse prances through Padstow's narrow streets, the musicians singing and playing, the dancer waving his club. The whole town follows on behind, the dancers finishing up at Prideaux Place to be welcomed by the Squire and his family. Originally a monastic tithe barn, Prideaux Place is now a fine Elizabethan house built about the time of the Armada, with a deer park overlooking the estuary.

The Hobby-Horse has even taken part in international folk-days at the Royal Albert Hall.

10.
WRECK IN THE CAMEL ESTUARY

It was a novel experience boarding the wreck on the Doom Bar near Polzeath. In 1939 when we first saw it, it had presumably only recently been thrown up on the rocky shore.

   We trekked across the rocks to explore its interior, and walking the deck, there was the strange sensation of movement, as though the ship were still afloat – a result of the angle at which it was lying.

   Years later, it was a surprise to see the wreck still there – though reduced by time and tide to mere rusted remains.

Visiting wreck
off Polzeath, 1939.

11.
MORE BURIED CHURCHES

Innumerable coves and wide stretches of sand are a feature of both north and south coasts of Cornwall – though, in general, the north coast, with its majestic cliff scenery, is more spectacular than the milder south. From the cliff-tops one can look down 500 feet or more to where the Atlantic breakers pound the tumbled rocks, and the wild restless seas surge up deep, sandy-floored gullies. North-westerly gales have swept thousands of tons of sand over some northerly areas, notably Holywell Bay, near Perranporth, and Harlyn and Constantine Bay, which are the districts of the sand-dunes – or towans, as they are called.

On a hot sunny day in August 1938, we set out from the village of Cubert (lying between Newquay and Perranporth) to visit St Piran's (or Perran) Oratory. At that time, there was a guide to show one the way,

Setting off for St Piran's Oratory, 1938. (Guide on right and his dog)

and, accompanied by the man and his dog, we trekked across a desert-like waste until we came to this most venerated of Cornish shrines, sometimes called the 'lost church' or St Piran's Oratory Chapel.

Said to be the earliest Christian building remaining in Cornwall and attributed to the ninth or tenth centuries, it was be-lieved to stand on the site of the original chapel of St Piran which probably dated from the fifth or sixth century. A small rectangular building, 25ft long by 12ft wide, it was covered over by sand for 300 years or more, only coming to light

St Piran's Cross.

around 1830 when the dunes shifted. When we saw it that day in 1938, it had been covered over with a protective shell and was kept locked.

Another church, built some 300 yards away on the other side of a stream, became threatened by sand at the end of the 1700s and was rebuilt at Lambourne about three miles away. Parts of the old church were incorporated into the new and vestiges of the ruined walls remained.

In the 1980s we set out to look for the Oratory Chapel again and eventually found someone able to direct us to the starting point. White marker-stones replaced the guide of former years, and following them we rediscovered this, in retrospect, most romantic spot. It was somewhat disappointing, however, to find that the chapel, suffering from flooding and vandalism, had recently been filled in again on the advice of the Department of the Environment. Only a stone plaque now marks the spot, though the ruined walls, somewhat reduced since last seen, still remain.

On Trixie and Baal at Holywell Bay, 1938.

In the dunes nearby stands the cross of St Piran. Said to be one of the most ancient in Cornwall and mentioned in a charter of King Edgar in A.D. 960, it was, even at that time, an old landmark.

It is believed that another cell built by St Piran once existed at Perranuthnoe, situated above Perran Sands by Mount's Bay. If so, it must now lie under the sea, for the coastline in these parts has been eroded away by about a mile since those days. The church here is dedicated to St Piran, and also to St Michael – both contenders for the title of patron saint of Cornwall. St Piran was one of at least one hundred Celtic saints who came as missionaries to Cornwall from Ireland and Wales and who gave their names to Cornish villages and churches. The patron saint of tinners, he was said to have been the first to discover the art of tin-smelting.

Other memories of our stay at Cubert were our frequent visits to Holywell Bay – though, on a recent visit, it was not as remembered due to a huge sandbank blocking the view of the beach. Apart from the inevitable swimming and surfing, there was another attraction, the two horses, Baal and Trixie (mother and daughter) owned by an elderly man (well, he seemed elderly to us) who gave pony rides. Many were the times my sister and I thudded the length of the beach, benefiting from his tuition as he showed us how to hold the reins, how to grip with knees and ankles, and how to trot. In the end, we became such good customers that we were given free rides.

The village itself has grown considerably since those days, making it difficult to connect it with the little place we once knew.

Lanlovey Farm, Cubert.

Cubert Church.

Ellenglaze, Cubert, 1938.

Mr. Proudfoot, The Retreat, Cubert, 1938.

Mrs. Phillips, Ellenglaze, 1938.

12.
BEDRUTHAN STEPS

Having enjoyed pre-war bathing on this spectacular, much-photographed beach, one has noted in recent times that even access to the beach has been banned for safety reasons.

More recently, the steps leading down to the beach have been re-opened, though bathing is still prohibited.

According to legend, the enormous rocks standing around on the beach were a giant's stepping-stones.

High tide at Bedruthan Steps, 1939.

13.
NEWQUAY

Considered by many to be first amongst Cornwall's holiday resorts, Newquay with its wonderful sandy beaches attracts thousands of visitors during the summer months.

In the mid-1500s Newquay was a port, and in 1838 a new quay was built for the exportation of china clay. The pilchard fishing industry flourished from the seventeenth century onwards, and a feature of the resort from early times is the old Huer's Hut on the headland. From this vantage post, the huer would watch for signs of approaching pilchard 'schools' out in the bay. On noting a discoloration of the sea marking the arrival of a shoal, he would shout "Hevva! Hevva!" through his trumpet to alert the local fishermen.

Still a landmark, the huer's hut with its thick stone walls stands firm and solid on the cliff-top, castellated and dazzling white in the

Huer's Hut, Newquay.

Coast to the North, Porth.

sunshine against the blue of the bay. Diamond-shaped peep-holes face towards the sea, and a flight of worn steps above is the huer's platform.

Porth's beautiful beach is well remembered, with Porth Island joined to it by a high bridge. Meeting up with friends on a pre-war visit, it was of particular interest to be shown the enormous cave known as the Banqueting Hall, in which unusual venue concerts used to be held, so we were told. What was the seating accommodation like, one wondered.

Looking into the Banqueting Hall, 1938.

Bridge, Porth.

14.
ST IVES

This picturesque small town with its ancient cottages, granite courts and alleyways is at its best in winter when the visitors have departed and only the fishermen and artists remain. In summer it is – sadly – a place to be avoided, due to the crowds which throng its little crooked streets. Which is perhaps why our visits there were few and far between, though pre-war St Ives must surely have been a lot less crowded than it is today.

The old grey town is built on a narrow neck of land between two bays and is surrounded by water on three sides. Backed by rising hills, it lies close to the water's edge, the vivid blue of the sea on a fine day being remarkable. The harbour is alive with the comings and goings of fishing and pleasure boats.

St Ives takes its name from St Ia the Virgin, one of twenty-six children of King Brechan. Most of them arrived in Cornwall miraculously, crossing the sea on millstones or in granite troughs or, as in the case of St Ia, lightly wafted by the breeze as she stood perched on a cabbage

St Ives and Porthminster Sands, early twentieth century.

Out fishing, 1939.

leaf. The bones of St Ia are said to be buried somewhere beneath the church.

On 4th September 1775, John Wesley preached at St Ives "in the little meadow above the town". He recorded in his diary that "the people in general here (excepting the rich) seem almost persuaded to be Christians."

Farther back in time, the family of Tregose (or Tregosse) was one of the oldest in the neighbourhood of St Ives, the name appearing in the Subsidy Roll of 1327. A descendant, Thomas Tregoss, son of William Tregoss of St Ives, strictly brought up by Puritan parents, was "thrust in as Puritan preacher" at the church, the vicar having been ejected. He subsequently transferred to Mylor (then 'Miler') and was himself ejected from the living in August 1660 as being "not ordained and unwilling to conform to the articles and the liturgy". Continuing to preach, he was committed to Launceston gaol for three months, and following a period of "deep despondency", broke into Mabe church, mounting the pulpit and haranguing the congregation. Arrested and imprisoned again at Launceston, he was released shortly afterwards. After which he invaded Mabe church twice more and was gaoled at Launceston and Bodmin but immediately set free. In prison at Exeter, he was once again bailed out. He died at Penryn in January 1672.

15.
WHERE MERMAIDS SING

The coastline from Land's End to St Ives is a wild and exposed one, and the day of our visit to Gurnard's Head was wet and windy – judging from the photographs taken on that occasion, which show us well wrapped up against the elements. This fantastic outcrop of rock, which is one of the wildest headlands in the country, appears idyllic in brilliant sunshine; though it is a different story with the sun shrouded in mist and a ship's siren wailing like a banshee.

Situated 'twixt sea and moor, the little granite village of Zennor with its small twelfth-century church surrounded by granite houses and a pattern of tiny, stone-walled fields, goes back to the Iron Age. On entering the churchyard, one pauses to read a memorial stone dedicated to a certain John Davey, who died in 1891 and who – according to the inscription – was the last person in the county to have an extensive knowledge of the Cornish language. Which puts one in mind of the famous Dolly Pentreath of Mousehole who was the last person actually to speak Cornish as her native tongue. It is remarkable that in recent years there has been a revival of the Cornish language, which pre-dates historic records, and is said to have much in common with the language of Brittany. In some places it is being used from time to time during church services.

Inside the church one discovers the fa-mous Mermaid Chair situated in the side chapel. The sides of the chair are two bench-ends preserved from the restoration of 1890, and legend says that a beautiful woman wear-ing a long robe used to sit at the back of the church listening to the singing of a chorister named Matthew Trewhella. One evening she

A chilly August day at Gurnard's Head. 1934.

Zennor.

succeeded in luring him down to a little stream running through the village and together they followed it into the sea at Pendour Cove. Legend has it that should you go to the Mermaid's Cove, as it has become known, on a warm summer's night and listen carefully, you might even hear the pair singing together.

The figure of the mermaid on the bench-end (she is no beauty) could be 500 or 600 years old, though the date is uncertain. In her left hand she holds a large comb and in her right a glass. Out of place as these creatures may seem in a church, their half-human, half-fish appearance was supposed to represent the divinity and humanity of Christ. It is noteworthy that the Mermaid of Zennor is the only mermaid mentioned by name in the Encyclopaedia Britannica.

Three cross-heads exist in the churchyard, the Cornish cross being a familiar feature of the Cornish landscape. In older times, twelve stood either side of the path running across the fields from St Ives to Zennor, at each of which the coffin-bearers would stop to ease their burden on the trek to the church. The head of the Cornish cross displayed in a garden in the village bears a notice to the effect that it became split at the back whilst in the making and was never completed or used. Crosses of this type date back to the ninth century and were erected as acts of piety, usually marking church paths.

The first church at Zennor would probably have been built during the sixth and seventh centuries, when an influx into Cornwall of Celtic Christianity from Brittany and Ireland took place. Two ruined chapels exist in the parish, one at Gurnard's Head, the other in a field with the intriguing name of 'Pit Poy'. Above, on the wild granite moors lies Zennor Quoit – a chambered tomb dating from as long ago as 3000 B.C.

On display in the village is the Zennor Plague stone, which was placed in its present position at the boundary of Zennor during outbreaks of the dread disease. It was the practice to fill the depression in the centre of these stones with vinegar to disinfect money that changed hands between villagers and outsiders. The main cholera epidemics in Cornwall took place between 1832 and 1849.

The narrow coast road from Gurnard's Head finds its way over wild, high-rising moorland country where craggy cliffs plunge steeply to the sea, and great boulders lie strewn around. Contin-

Sennen Cove, 1934.

uing southwards, one passes through the mining towns of Pendeen and St Just-in-Penwith by Cape Cornwall, until one reaches Sennen, where granite cliffs give way to the shell-covered beach aptly named Whitesand Bay. In bygone days, one could have imagined the area to be the haunt of witches.

Indeed, at Sennen (known as the 'last village in England') the old lady clad all in black, wearing a hat resembling a witch's headgear, seemed to fit the part. When she invited us into her little whitewashed cottage, we complied with some unease; though all was well, and we were impressed by the numerous trophies which cluttered her tiny living-room, taken from wrecks by her seafaring forebears.

Many years after that pre-war visit, we were surprised to learn that our 'old' friend had not been so elderly after all. In fact, at that time she was probably just a young woman. Immediately recognising our description of the lady in question (Old Annie, as she was known), a local inhabitant told us that she had only recently died. She had always dressed in black apparently, which contributed to the impression of advanced years.

SOUTH CORNWALL

16.
LAND'S END

Standing on the cliff-top, looking out to sea through his binoculars, and studying the ship making its way across the ocean, my father turned to remark on its size to the couple standing nearby. On doing so, he – and they – were amazed to discover that they were well-acquainted, being from our home-town of Poole. Quite a coincidence in such a sparsely-populated spot.

Nowadays, sadly, Land's End is somewhat less sparsely-populated, and very far from being the peaceful spot it once was.

The First and Last House is still there, of course – if you can find it.

'First and Last House in England', Land's End – 31st August, 1934.

17.
THE LOGAN ROCK

On the ancient cliff fort of Treen Castle near Land's End stands this famous rock calculated to weigh eighty or ninety tons. So exactly poised was it that it is said that anyone, applying his shoulder to it, could make the whole mass rock. In a high wind it was even seen rolling on its pivot.

On 8th April 1824, the Logging (rocking) Stone was forced from its equilibrium "through the excessive vibration given to it by the united manual exertions of nine persons". A party of sailors belonging to H.M. cutter 'Nimble', commanded by a certain Lieutenant Goldsmith, son of Oliver Goldsmith, came ashore for the purpose of removing it from its situation. They were successful in this act of vandalism, but failed in their attempt, the stone being restored to its former situation on 2nd November following. This took place by means of the skilful application of machinery

Logan Rock being restored, 1824.

| Astride the Logan Rock, 1934. | Sitting in the Giant's Armchair. |

and by the labour of upwards of fifty persons under the sole direction of Lieutenant Goldsmith R.N. himself. For, having been party to its disturbance, he was compelled to replace it at his own expense. Sad to say, it never rocked so easily again.

On a recent visit, it was a surprise to see climbers arrive equipped with all the necessary gear for a stiff ascent. Pre-war memories of the Logan Rock include climbing it unaided, as the above photographs confirm.

According to legend, if any woman wished to become a witch like Madgy Figgy, all she had to do was to touch the rock nine times at midnight.

Opposite Treen is lovely Porthcurno with its white-sanded, safe bathing beach, and up on the edge of the cliff the Minack Open-air Theatre.

18.
HIDDEN TREASURE

An intriguing pastime for pre-war visitors to Cornwall – now unfortunately no longer widely practised – was searching for semi-precious stones
on the beaches. Penzance was a popular location, and the sight of folk
scanning the pebbles as they tramped the seashore was a fairly common
one. Stones most usually sought were the more familiar and easily-
distinguishable ones and included crystal, topaz, rose quartz, amethyst,
agate, carnelian and onyx – in the rough, of course.

Once one understood what to look for, odd moments searching for
good specimens often yielded dividends; for, with so many examples lying
around, they were not difficult to find. (One can tread on pieces of crystal
and topaz, even rose quartz, while walking along a Cornish country lane;
they are not confined to the beaches). Having selected and filled the
beach-bag with the best specimens one could find, one would adjourn to
the gem (or 'stone' shop as we called it) situated on the promenade at
Penzance. Here experts would make a rapid assessment, throwing out the
inferior and retaining only the best. After which there was a choice as to
the finished article required; a necklace (five stones on a silver chain) at a
cost of 7/6d; a pendant on a silver chain, 5/-; or rings, brooches and
cuff-links at 2/6d each. Ready for collection in a few days, cut, polished
and mounted, they made ideal Christmas gifts. Not only were they
excellent value by today's standards, but there was also the satisfaction of
having found one's own raw material.

Sadly, the war put an end to treasure-hunting on Cornish beaches,
except, that is, for those fortunate enough to have their own stone-cutting
equipment. Today gem shops (including the one at Penzance) sell only
ready-made jewellery, even the lumps of rock displayed in the windows
probably being imported from abroad. Nowadays, whenever I hear of
crystal quartz and topaz (milky-white and yellow-tinged respectively in the

Rose quartz necklace + topaz, crystal
and moss-agate pendants.

raw), my mind goes back to the beach at Penzance. The light mauve amethyst (clouded) was also easily recognisable, as was the pinky hue of the rose quartz – the deeper the better. Onyx, carnelian, agate, and moss agate were also eagerly sought; though we could not lay claim to having found the lump of Connemara marble washed over from Ireland and converted into yet another five-stone necklace.

Why should Cornwall be so rich in treasure? Briefly, it is generally believed that after the original volcanic land surface of this particular part of the country had formed and hardened, there were further movements caused by shrinkage of the Earth's crust These produced cracks into which flowed boiling liquids rising from inside the Earth. After many years the liquids hardened, and as they cooled they formed crystal.

Cornwall is rich in minerals too, and at St Michael's Mount are to be found a greater number and variety of rare and interesting examples per cubic foot than in any other area of equivalent size on the whole globe.

In fact, where both minerals and metals are concerned, Cornwall is said to be one of the richest places in the world.

19.
SANCREED

The attractive little village of Sancreed lies off the beaten track, roughly mid-way between Penzance and St Just. Two or three years ago – for this was a more recent discovery – it was intriguing to find, in the churchyard, an ancient Cornish Cross thought to date from around the tenth century. Slightly leaning, it is remarkable for being one of only a few in existence having a sculptured figure, representing Christ in Glory, on its cross head. Parts of the cross shaft were found within the church wall and the cross head in the boundary wall; they were brought together and set up in the churchyard in 1894. The inscription at the base of the shaft is believed to be the signature of the sculptor.

Of interest inside the old church is the alms box of date 1739, provided in accordance with an injunction of Queen Elizabeth I in 1559.

These alms boxes, of which quite a number remain today, were known as 'The Poor Man's Box or Chest'. Later ones were carved or made of metal (as is this one), or even of stone.

On a lighter note, it was interesting to learn that in 1667 parishioners took the drastic step of pulling the parson (probably a 'usurper' as no vicar appears to have been in possession at the time) from the pulpit, and took action against him in the Bishop's Court for "making jokes at their expense in his sermons".

Ancient Cross, Sancreed -
with figure of Christ.

20.
ST MICHAEL'S MOUNT

It was a memorable experience attending morning service in the chapel on St Michael's Mount one Sunday morning. Members of the St Leven family were present, also one of the future Queen's Ladies-in-waiting.

Particularly remembered was the steep ascent to the Mount, and the manner in which we travelled there and back – on foot across the causeway on the outward journey, by boat an hour or so later when the tide had turned.

At Marazion, we enjoyed a moonlight bathe – one of the warmest ever remembered.

St Michael's Mount, showing the houses of employees on the Mount, 1934.

21.
WESTWARDS BY TRAIN

Our annual pre-war holiday in the delectable duchy of Cornwall is always a much looked-forward-to event. It is also inevitably prefaced by the long, eight-hour train journey from Dorset.

Our trunks having been duly dispatched in advance, we set off by taxi, encumbered only by Father's ancient 'Swift' bicycle – and hand-luggage, including Mother's hat-box. We are dropped at Poole Station – more imposing than the present-day substitute – and having purchased newspapers and comics at the bookstall, we await with keen anticipation the arrival of the steam-train. It roars towards us, emitting fumes, and as it thunders by we scan it eagerly for an empty compartment. Then on we pile – with the exception of Father who has gone to the luggage-van to check that his bicycle of ancient vintage is not left standing on the platform. The guard blows his whistle, doors slam, and we gaze anxiously from the window. Will Father make it, we wonder.

But here he is and all is well. In the nick of time we haul him aboard. Light-hearted as a schoolboy released from school, he tosses his hat onto the luggage-rack and takes a corner seat, back to the engine. The train blasts shrilly and lurches forward. It gathers speed and we are on our way.

Our first stop is Templecombe in Somerset, where it is "All Change". We alight and the bicycle routine takes place in reverse. A station notorious for its lengthy waits, it nevertheless affords opportunity for stretching the legs. On this occasion the boredom is relieved by an unusual spectacle. An escaped calf cavorts along the track (unelectrified) and the subsequent chase up the line to recapture it is a welcome diversion.

The train arrives at last, the bicycle is safely aboard, and so are we. Further cause for anxiety presents itself now, however, for Father appears to have mislaid the tickets. Goggle-eyed, we children hold our breath whilst he makes the usual leisurely search through his pockets. We relax as the tickets surface, and settle down with papers and comics – or doze, or watch the countryside flash past.

Exeter St David's is the next stop, involving rapid transference from one platform to another. Helpful porters dexterously manoeuvre trolleys piled high with baggage, relieving owners of much strain. As the train thunders in, the crowd surges forward and we hasten aboard. Doors slam shut, but horror of horrors, Father, gone on his usual errand of checking his velocipede, is nowhere in sight. We lean from the window and scan the platform with growing apprehension, the guard blows his whistle and the train inches slowly out of the station. Round-eyed with alarm, we look at Mother who appears pale and anxious, for no Father, no tickets! Ten fraught minutes later he appears and calms our fears. The explanation is simple. Having nipped into the luggage-van at the last minute, along with the bike, he has reached us by way of the corridor. We breathe again and settle down.

Later, as the train rumbles across the Tamar, we children rush to the window to catch a glimpse of its tail-end as it rounds the bend. Over the border now and in Cornwall, we sense once more that indefinable air of magic. For this is 'foreign' territory and we are aware of that strange, all-pervasive sense of other-worldliness.

Our final change, when travelling to Porthleven, is the little wayside station of Gwinear Road,* and from here to Helston our journey (one that can no longer be taken by train) is slow, punctuated by a stop at every station. What strange-sounding names those stations have, notably Doublebois and Nancegollen, the latter derived, according to legend, from the elderly rustic who drove his one and only cow along the winding lanes, reciting as he went, "Nancy, go alon'; Nancy, go alon'!"

---

* This station, first opened on 8th May 1887, was once the main-line link for the Helston branch. Today all signs of the station have gone, only some rusty railings remaining.

Porthleven, 1934.

Helston at last, and we alight. Father's Swift bicycle stands safe and sound on the platform, along with Mother's hat-case and the two hefty cabin-trunks sent on in advance. Father goes through his pockets to locate the tickets, and we fall into a waiting taxi. The journey behind us and the little fishing village of Porthleven ahead, we settle down to happy anticipation of yet another unforgettable holiday in the delectable duchy of Cornwall.

Porthleven harbour, 1935.

22.
PORTHLEVEN

Pre-war holidays spent at Porthleven with our kind landlady, Mrs Bessie Jenkin of 'Tremayno' on Breage Side (the house is still so named), are particularly memorable. And though recent visits have revealed changes, notably the departure of the pilchard-fishing industry to Newlyn (with the resultant disappearance of the familiar fishing fleet), the village remains basically the same.

On the road just above 'Tremayno' lived the mother of the well-known singer, Margaret Godley. When her daughter came to stay, it was a particular pleasure to hear her solos during the Sunday services at the local Methodist Chapel. There are two chapels in the village, the main one in Fore Street and the smaller Fisherman's Chapel up the hill at the back – though the latter is now no longer used. Although Church of England, we always attended the Fore Street Chapel, and sometimes my father (who was a clergyman) would be asked to preach there. He

Fore Street, Porthleven,
with methodist church top right.

Mrs Jenkin, outside 'Tremayno'.

Pre-war Porthleven, with 'Tremayno' in front, second from right.

preached at the Fisherman's Chapel too, and was even asked by the deacons if he would allow them to put him on their circuit.

On Sunday mornings and evenings after chapel, it was a frequent sight to see the fishermen gathered in groups on the quayside discussing the sermon. Sunday was strictly observed in Porthleven before the war. All shops closed, and the fishing-boats were taken into the inner harbour the previous evening. I well remember the occasion when some holiday-makers got into difficulties offshore in their yacht on a Sunday afternoon. The local fishermen gathered on the clifftop to watch their progress through binoculars. Having satisfied themselves that they were in no real danger, they would not go to their aid because it was the Sabbath. It was their own fault, they reckoned, for going out sailing on Sunday, and they could make their own way in. Times have changed somewhat!

We got to know some of the 'locals' well during our several visits to the village, including the Cowl family who owned the newsagent's shop on the opposite side of the harbour. Also Mrs Jenkin's brother-in-law, Mr Sam Jenkin, who lived next door to 'Tremayno' (which is semi-detached) with his wife. The family suffered a tragedy one year with the loss of two brothers in a fishing disaster. Other well-remembered local personalities were the twins, two elderly men who were often to be seen sitting side-by-side on a seat ocpposite the bus stop. When one looked left, so did

Out fishing with
Sam Jenkin, the
Jeyes boys and
Mrs Castellano,
1934.

More fishing,
with our
friends, the
Jeyes, 1934.

the other; when one blew his nose, the other did too.

Sometimes Sam Jenkin would take us out in his boat mackerel-fishing, and to feel the tug of a fish on the end of a running line was always a great thrill. On one occasion I landed an 8lb. pollock. I do not recall that the sight of the poor creatures flapping about on the bottom of the boat affected me greatly, though nowadays I would probably enjoy the spectacle less.

And talking of fish, my sister and I would often get up early and go down to the quay below 'Tremayno' where the fishing-boats had just come in after a night's fishing. The fishermen would throw us some pilchards, which we would take back to Mrs Jenkin to cook for breakfast.

Lizard lifeboat, 'Southern King', at Porthleven,
new in 1934, cost £8,000.

There is, in my opinion, nothing quite like fresh pilchards, or fresh mackerel liberally besprinkled with lemon. Other culinary delights remembered were delicious fresh lobster and crab – straight from the sea – salads, and huge bowls of Cornish cream on the table for supper; also Mrs Jenkin's wonderful home-made pasties, full of meat and vegetables, which we took with us on our trips out for the day.

Another 'treat' was a trip round the bay on the Lizard lifeboat when it made a visit to Porthleven for the purpose. I well recall the smooth polished sheen of its woodwork, and the red woollen hats worn by the crew. Also being told that if the lifeboat were to become split in two, both halves would float.

On a somewhat gruesome note, there was the occasion when the body of a man in bathing trunks was towed into the harbour. Mrs Jenkin had introduced us to the Eddy family of Glanith Farm, Prospidnick, and, at the instigation of their daughter Marion (of similar age to ourselves), we

At Mr Eddy's farm, Glanith, Prospidnick, nr Porthleven.

children, possessed of a ghoulish curiosity, lost no time in going down to the quay to inspect the body. I remember that, due to it having been in the water for several weeks, the flesh had become jelly-like, identification being only possible when it was discovered that the man had one finger missing.

We spent happy times at Glanith Farm, riding in the horse-drawn trap or on horseback. Members of the Eddy family still live in the area, and it was interesting to meet up with them again in recent years.

Up the old pilchard lookout, 1934.

Another well-remembered event was the arrival of the German timber boat, the 'Aar' from Hamburg, in August 1935. It remained docked in the harbour for several days, during which time it was a source of particular interest to my sister and myself. Little did we think that in four years' time we would be at war with that nation.

The regatta was another memorable feature of our holiday, the greasy pole being conveniently sited on the rocks just below 'Tremayno'. Yet another highlight was the swimming pool, a natural pool in the rocks below the cliffs at Porthleven, the far end of

which was concreted to keep the
water in. It was quite deep enough
for children to learn to swim in, and
this I lost no time in doing. Many,
many happy hours were spent in
that pool, though on a recent return
visit to Porthleven, there was difficulty in locating it. For in the intervening years the concrete had en-

German timber boat, 'The Aar' from
Hamburg, Porthleven, 1935.

tirely disappeared, worn away by the action of the sea.

Another pastime much enjoyed was fishing in rock-pools with a
rod and line, the bait used being limpet. We soon discovered that there
was quite an art in knocking limpets off the rocks, as, if one were not quick
about it, the limpet would tighten its grip and would be impossible to
dislodge. Scooping out the inside of a limpet is not something which
would hold much appeal nowadays, though as children we took it in our
stride.

Those rock-pools with their seaweed, crabs, and anemones were a
real fascination, while the swimming-pool was a boon. For the only other
beach at Porthleven is the long stretch of shingle on the far side of the
harbour, steeply shelving and with an undertow which makes it unsafe for
bathing at any time. We were told of a honeymoon couple who, as soon as
they arrived in the village, went swimming off this particular beach (in
spite of being warned not to do so) and were drowned. In more recent
times, there have been reports of a man shooting himself on the rocks by
the old life-boat slip just below 'Tremayno', and of another committing
suicide by jumping off the end of the pier. In fact, over the years fatalities
at Porthleven have cropped up from time to time on the news, one of the
most recent involving a boy who, with his father, ventured onto the pier
during a storm. Sadly, the boy was washed over into the sea and drowned.

Even on wet days, of which there was the occasional one during
our month's holiday, we never suffered from boredom. Even if unable to

go out, there was an excellent view of the harbour from our sitting-room, and always something of interest to watch as the boats came and went, tossing up and down on the choppy grey water.

One afternoon, Mrs Jenkin took us to a summer fête at Godolphin House situated inland from Mount's Bay between Townshend and Godolphin Cross. A house has existed here from very early times and the present building has been described as "marvellously evocative of the Cornish past". Dating from the fifteenth century, it has Elizabethan additions, the unique north front, supported on massive granite columns, having been built about 1635 over the Elizabethan gateway.

The founder of the fortunes of the famous Godolphin family was Sir John Godolphin, Sheriff of Cornwall in 1504. The family owned the house up to the latter part of the eighteenth century, and many well-known family members were born there. Sidney Godolphin was killed at Chagford during the Civil War, and another Sidney, a friend of the Duke of Marlborough and the first Earl of Godolphin, was Queen Anne's Lord High Treasurer. Sidney's son, Francis, the second and last Earl, married Henrietta Churchill, Marlborough's daughter, and became governor of the Isles of Scilly. He painted the picture of the famous stallion, the Godolphin Arab, which hangs in the dining-room at Godolphin House.

Prince Charles (later to become Charles II) is said to have stayed at Godolphin House during his escape to the Scillies, and a large room on the west side of the courtyard has always been known as the 'King's Room'.

A grandson of Sir Francis was Sir William Godolphin of Treve-neag, who became captain of the Isles of Scilly. He died in 1696 in the parish of Mabe, and left money in his will for the founding of the Godolphin Schools at Hammersmith and Salisbury. The Godolphin family were patrons of the living of Breage, mention of which reminds one of the sailor's popular prayer:

> *"God keep us from rocks and shelving sands,*
> *And save us from Breage and Germoe men's hands."*

23.
CUT OFF BY THE TIDE!

Amongst numerous happy childhood memories of holidays in Cornwall, one strikes a less pleasant chord. On a hot sunny day in August many years ago, the treachery of the sea around the Cornish coast was brought home to us in no uncertain terms.

My parents, sister and I had set out for a walk along the cliffs lying west of Porthleven, well-equipped with stout shoes and walking-sticks for a rough cliff ramble. The springy turf was littered with sea-pinks, and the fields beyond the low stone walls were dotted with sheep. Craggy cliffs descended to tiny deserted coves inhabited only by sea-birds and it was when a rough track winding down to a long stretch of untrodden white sand came into view, that the decision was made to abandon our cliff walk. My father said the tide would be going out for some time, and he was usually right about such things.

The descent to the beach safely accomplished, we walked its length with only the gulls for company. Rounding a headland, we crossed another beach and yet another, finally arriving at a rocky gully stretching from the tide-line to the foot of the cliff. Being empty, it was negotiated without difficulty, and it was not until we reached the far end of that stretch of sand that we made an alarming discovery. Time had sped by without our realising it; the tide had turned and was coming in fast around the headland. We stood looking in alarm as breakers rushed in over the jagged granite rocks, surging into an ever-deepening pool at the base of the cliff. To climb those slippery, mussel-covered rocks to reach the next cove was out of the question.

So we hastily retraced out steps, my sister running on ahead across the ever-narrowing stretch of sand. In my mind's eye I can see her now, standing by the gully, arms extended to indicate the depth of water in it. As we joined her, the sight was awesome. Breakers pounded up the

The cliffs at Porthleven - scene of our adventure.

rapidly-filling gulf right to the foot of the cliff and the sea grew more turbulent by the minute. We were well and truly cut off, without a soul in sight to witness our predicament.

We scanned the cliffs, but there was no clearly-defined path – no path at all, in fact – to the top. It might have been possible to climb to a sufficient height to put ourselves out of reach of the rising sea, but this would have entailed a wait of many hours until the tide went down again.

So the decision was made and into the gully we went. Neither of us children could stand, so Mother took charge of my sister, Father of me, and firmly grasped, I seemed to glide effortlessly along – a phenomenon which I think had little to do with any attempts to swim – though, having just learned the art, surely this was as good a time as any to put it to the test!

My parents, impeded by sticks and walking shoes (which had not been abandoned) made slow progress, for the uneven floor of the gully ensured that one was elevated one minute, down in the depths the next. Mother, nearer to the sea, fared better, for out there the bottom of the gully was flatter and sandier; though the water was deeper, as she discovered when a wave washed over her shoulders. In mid-stream and with great presence of mind, she handed her wrist-watch to Father for safe-keeping in one of his pockets. Ironically, it was ruined, though his own watch suffered no ill effects.

And so we reached safety and hauled ourselves out thankfully onto the rocks – apart from Father, that is, whose flannel trousers were so weighted with sea-water that it took the combined efforts of the three of us to get him up. Yet we had made it, complete with gear; but would there be any more hazards ahead, we asked ourselves as we began the long trek home.

All was well, however, though on arriving at the 'home' beach, we did feel somewhat foolish, wondering what folk sunning themselves on the rocks would make of our wet and bedraggled appearance. No one appeared to notice, however; though on entering the village there was bewilderment on the face of the elderly lady leaning over her garden gate.

"We've been for a swim in our clothes!" Father told her, his sense of humour undiminished.

Back at our 'digs', our kind landlady's first reaction was amusement, which quickly turned to alarm when she realised that we were not joking. She should have warned us, she said, dismayed, for we were not the first to have been cut off on that treacherous stretch of coast where the tide can turn so quickly.

And that was not the last we were to hear of our adventure. An account of it appeared in the local newspaper the following week, and we acquired even wider fame when the Manchester *Guardian* got hold of the story. Following which, friends living in the north wrote enquiring what we had been up to.

Well – we had learned our lesson and such a mishap would not occur again.

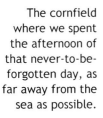

The cornfield where we spent the afternoon of that never-to-be-forgotten day, as far away from the sea as possible.

24.
MORE ANCIENT CUSTOMS

Just as with the coming of spring the Celts rejoiced at the return to life of the god of vegetation, so in the autumn they mourned his death. An old Cornish rhyme which used to be sung by the reapers as they cut the last sheaf is a survival of this ancient custom:

"I'll have un, I'll have un, I'll have un,
What have 'e, What have 'e, What have 'e,
What will 'e, What will 'e, What will 'e
Onec, Onec, Onec, O'hurro, O'hurro, O'hurro!"

As the apparently meaningless piece of doggerel was repeated, the farmer would wave a sheaf in the air whilst the harvesters stood around in a circle. The chanting in the harvest field was said to be so mournful that it is thought to have originated as a song of lamentation. The custom was not confined to Cornwall either, but was very widespead throughout the country and even the world.

The Druids or Celtic priests knew quite a lot about astronomy and used stone circles – many of which survive to this day – for the purpose of observing the stars. They would notice how the rising or setting sun and certain heavenly bodies lined up with a central stone and a particular stone on the circumference of the circle. In this way, they were able to calculate the passing of time, the seasons of the year, and the dates on which their festivals fell.

One such ancient circle, which stood on Trewarvas Head near Porthleven, was unfortunately destroyed towards the end of the nineteenth century by someone who hoped to find treasure hidden beneath the huge stones. From the top of the high cliff where the circle was situated, the Druids would have had wonderful views seaward and would probably have spent the long hours of a starlit night making their observations.

On the summit of another Cornish elevation known as Tregoning Hill in the parish of Breage, they would light a great fire on Midsummer Eve, a custom which survived almost into the twentieth century. In bygone ages, it seems likely that human victims would have been sacrificed at this festival in honour of the sea, in the hope of warding off God's anger from the community. It seems that this same custom was observed in the remoter parts of the Scottish Islands and Highlands right down to the beginning of the eighteenth century, human sacrifices appearing to have played a part.

MORE PORTHLEVEN MEMORIES – 1937

Carnival.

Aquatic sports.

25.
HELSTON

Memories of Helston include Monday morning visits to the cattle market, and walking back to Porthleven three miles away through the lovely Penrose Walk. Loe Pool, fed by the little river Camber and backed by the pebble and sandy ridge known as Loe Bar, appeared somewhat silent and sinister as we passed it, and it still does.

Here, on the 29th December 1807, occurred a major disaster when the frigate, H.M.S. *Anson*, was cast up on its shore with the loss of 100 lives, including some children and the captain, who stayed with the ship until the end. Amongst the crowd looking helplessly on was one, Henry Trengrouse, born at Helston on 18th March 1772. Descended from a family having long associations as freeholders of the town, his father was Nicholas Trengrouse (1739-1814) and his mother, Mary, née Williams. Henry was educated at Helston Grammar School and became a cabinet-maker.

The dire tidings that a large frigate had been driven onto Loe Bar soon spread around the town that day, and Trengrouse, along with many others, hastened to the scene. On that fateful day, buffeted by a gale from the west-south-west, the captain had decided to run to port. Heading for Land's End which he mistook for the Lizard, he resolved to beach the ship on sand off Loe Pool but, with a horrendous sea running, it heeled over broadside. Fortunately the main mast formed a floating raft over which most of those who survived were able to escape.

Trengrouse returned home drenched to the skin and sick at heart, and was confined to bed for nearly a week with a severe cold. The tragic event made a lasting impression which he could not get out of his mind. Watching a rocket soar high into the sky during a firework display to mark the king's birthday, an idea occurred to him. Could not this be the means of carrying a rope to a sinking vessel, thus providing a means of escape for those in distress, he asked himself.

From then onwards he laboured on his scheme, expending £3,000 on experiments and sacrificing his health, his capital and his business in the process. Success came at last, though he was to experience many a setback as he spent the rest of his life endeavouring to interest successive governments in his invention.

Yet his last words to his son before his death in 1854 were, "If you live to be as old as I am, you will find my rocket apparatus all along our shores." His words proved true, for between 1870 and 1920 it was to be the means of saving 10,000 lives, and Trengrouse became known as 'The Sailors' Friend'.

Mention of Helston would, of course, be incomplete without reference to the Furry Dance for which the little town is world-famous.

Furry Dance, Helston.

26.
THE LIZARD

When one thinks of the Lizard Peninsula, one's mind goes back to the little workshops which lined the path down to the beach. Stocked with decorative and useful articles carved out of the serpentine stone, we found them fascinating. Lighthouses, fonts, eggcups and paperweights, down to small articles of jewellery, were on display and for sale. Still remembered, though long since gone, are the little serpentine rings bought for us children by our parents.

The workshops were a great attraction to the visitor, and it was intriguing to watch the stone-cutters, who made a living from the craft, working the stone. Serpentine, also known as the Lizard stone, varies from deep green streaked with wavy red and purple, to deep red mottled with lighter tones and veined with white. It is also to be found on Holy Island, Anglesey.

The workshops are still there, of course, though fewer in number nowadays. Any of the articles on display may be purchased.

* * * * * * *

Remembered too is the walk across the fields (on top of the wall for the youngsters) to picturesque Kynance Cove – a popular subject for photographers, as well as the scramble down to the beach; though, since the introduction in recent years of flights of wooden steps, it is no longer a scramble.

This lovely beach, or rather two beaches at low tide, was a favourite, though one has to be wary – for when the tide turns, the furthermost beach becomes completely cut off. On one occasion we witnessed an artist being rescued by boat. Perched on a rock engrossed in her painting, she had failed to notice the encroaching tide.

27.
ON GOONHILLY DOWN

High on the cliffs near Mullion, only a few miles from the Lizard Peninsula, where aerials today face towards the sky and turn to track the many satellites circling the Earth, exists a memorial. It is to the memory of Guglielmo Marconi (1874–1937) Italian physicist and radio pioneer who, at the age of twenty-one, successfully transmitted signals over two miles and sailed to England in order to file a patent. In this country, the shy little Italian carried out experiments at Poldhu Cove where, in 1901, he was able to send a message covering a distance of 198 miles between the Lizard and the Isle of Wight. In 1909 he won the Nobel prize for physics.

Soon afterwards, aerials were erected on both sides of the Atlantic and, despite trouble with gale-force winds, there were further successful transmissions. Wireless had come into its own and was to prove particularly advantageous to the Admiralty at the outbreak of the First World War. Some older residents of Helston still remember Marconi, whose yacht 'Elettra' – in effect a floating laboratory – was often to be seen in Mount's Bay. He stayed in Cornwall until 1935, after which he returned to Rome, where he died suddenly two years later.

All of which is a far cry from the famous Satellite Communications Earth Station which today lies off the Helston to St Keverne Road, on Goonhilly Down, and is one of Cornwall's most popular tourist attractions. Previously, the centre of operations had been Porthcurno, set in a se-

Path down to Kynance Cove - 1935.

cluded valley of gorse and bluebells on the Lizard Peninsula – a beach that in the mid-nineteenth century was rarely visited even by the locals, apart from a few pack-horses and farm carts going there to collect seaweed for the nearby farm. (On a return visit on a hot day in August recently, I found it to be far from deserted, the beach being packed with holidaymakers.)

In June 1870, however, surveyors and technicians from the English and Irish Magnetic Telegraph Company of London, financed by a cotton manufacturer, Lord Pender of Porthcurno, appeared on the scene. Until that time, attempts to lay sub-marine cables had not been successful, only short lengths working for limited periods being laid between the mainland and neighbouring islands. Then there came a breakthrough and soon cables were reaching out from Porthcurno (Port Kernow) to trading ports in many parts of the Empire and the world. With the opening of Goonhilly in 1970, the station ceased commercial operations, though the underseas cables network has been supplemented by multi-channel lines capable of carrying increased traffic.

Goonhilly has a number of distinctions to its name, being, for instance, the first station to possess two aerials on the same site, as well as the first to transmit live television programmes from Europe to America. The site was chosen because it possesses one of the warmest climates in the country and lacks electrical interference. On arrival at 'Telstar', as it is affectionately known to the locals (from the first ever satellite pictures on our television screens), one can view at close range the enormous saucers which, like the wind-farms at Delabole, are today a familiar feature of the Cornish landscape. As one enters the compound through its automatically controlled gates, one finds oneself in one of the largest and busiest Earth stations in the world.

So it is astonishing to be reminded that only 200 years ago the hangman's noose had dangled just yards away, in a place where robbers, bears and wolves roamed the rugged down at will.

In pitch darkness, one views complicated diagrams and visual aids, and television screens face one from all sides. An audio-visual show illustrates satellite technology and how it has evolved over the past twenty-five years or so, and as the talk proceeds one finds oneself intrigued, if somewhat blinded with science. An intricate system demonstrates

Goonhilly Satellite Station.

the complicated procedure set in train from the moment one picks up the telephone to make a call to a friend or business associate in America, or some other far-flung portion of the globe. In the observation tower one learns that the first aerial was completed at the station's establishment in July 1962, at which time there were only three aerials in the world. The Control Centre with its involved instrument panels constantly monitoring the satellite traffic is attended day and night right round the clock, television pictures being received here from all over the world. Big events such as royal tours abroad generate much activity.

Should all this strike a discordant note in a book dealing with the Cornwall of yesteryear, at least it highlights the contrasts between the then and now. However, the ghostly happenings reported to have occurred at Goonhilly since the Satellite Communications Earth Station came into being are perhaps more in keeping with the country's past. Ghost stories abound in the area, and those who man the satellite station at night can tell many a strange tale. Which to anyone who has seen the great luminous circles after dark, particularly by moonlight when they present an extraordinarily eerie aspect, comes as no surprise.

The Marconi Telegraph station at Porthcurno has now been dismantled and transferred to the Porthcurno Museum of Submarine Telegraphy, now open to the public. Here may be seen World War II tunnels which house the most important collection of communications equipment in the world.

28.
THE ROSELAND PENINSULA

With its many lovely beaches, miles of wonderful coastline and inland walks, this must be one of the most picturesque and unspoilt parts of the county and one which never seems to get crowded, even today.

One location stands out above all others – for, once seen, St Just-in-Roseland can surely never be forgotten. With its church perched at the river's edge and set amidst semi-tropical trees and shrubs, little changes here. Folk still pause to read the texts and quotations on the plaques bordering the pathway – amongst them:

> *"The kiss of the sun for pardon*
> *The song of the birds for mirth*
> *One is nearer God's heart in a garden*
> *Than anywhere else on earth."*

Two miles along the coast, St Mawes is chiefly remembered as a location popular with sailing enthusiasts, and for its castle built during the reign of Henry VIII as a defence against invasion by France. A ten-minute ferry-boat trip from St Mawes lands one at Place on St Anthony-in-Roseland – another peaceful, remote spot where a striking cream-coloured, grey-roofed mansion (once entirely grey) stands against a background of trees close to the estuary. Now privately-owned, The Place was

St Just-in-Roseland.

at one time a hotel, and – somewhat curiously – is joined at the rear to a now redundant church, the latter large and lofty and having a striking Norman doorway.

Of interest on the headland at St Anthony

The Place,
St Anthony-in-Roseland.

are the remains of the many fortifications forming the St Anthony Battery, an area used during World War I for army training. In World War II gun batteries were stationed here.

Other names from the past include Portscatho up the coast to the east, with extensive sandy beaches ideal for swimming, and still an active fishing village. At Gerrans a five-minute walk away at the top of the hill is a church with a medieval spire which has been a landmark to local sailors for generations.

As Cornish as one could wish for, is tiny Portloe, with cottages clustering around a harbour where boats land crabs and lobsters, and life goes on as if nothing in the world around had changed. Continuing on towards Dodman Point, Caerhays is remembered for its castle in a setting of 60 acres of woodland gardens containing roses, camellia and magnolia.

A more recent discovery was Veryan, well-kept and of much charm, a village notable for its four round-houses, two at each end, said to have been so built to prevent the devil lurking in the corners. Another recent discovery was Ruanlanihorne, with a church dedicated in 1321 to St Rumonus. It stands on the old coach road from Penzance to London. According to road maps of the late 1600s, the main road from London to Land's End ran through neighbouring Philleigh ('Philly' as it appears on an old map of 1695), crossing the river at the King Harry Ferry and Tolverne Passage.

29.
THE MANACLES

For centuries, a coal beacon burned on the headland at St Anthony-in-Roseland, marking the entrance to the Carrick Roads, keeping ships clear of the infamous Manacle Rocks.

Manacle bell buoy.

In 1834, a lighthouse took its place. The St Anthony Lighthouse is now automated, and frequently open to visitors during the summer months. It was the set for the television series, 'Fraggle Rock'.

MID-CORNWALL

30.
BODMIN MOOR

The most south-westerly moor of any size in Britain, Bodmin Moor with its bogs and pools rises to command fine views from its exposed and windswept granite tors. It was originally known as Fowey Moor, for the Fowey River rises in its high granite tors. Brown Willy and Rough Tor, its highest points, have been familiar landmarks from early days, as have the less scenic claypits of St Austell. Well remembered was the excitement of the small child on the train. "Oh look, Mummy, there's a big circus over there!" The 'circus' no longer exists, however, recent visits revealing an altered landscape of flattened peaks.

The moor affects some people strangely. A couple driving home to Fowey one winter's night were alarmed to see a white apparition looming up at the side of the road. It turned out to be nothing more sinister than a white horse looking over the hedge.

Jamaica Inn (should you stay there, you could well imagine that smugglers were coming to get you during the night), Bolventor, or Dozmary Pool – their very names are evocative of that other-worldliness that brooded over the Duchy in times past, and indeed still does. Dozmary Pool is notable for its legend of Tregeagle, the unjust steward, condemned forever to the task of emptying the bottomless pool of Dozmary with a holed limpet shell. Night and day, come rain or shine, he continued his hopeless task – but the pool never emptied, and one night, unable to stand it any longer, he fled howling and shrieking across the moor. So the story goes, at any rate.

31.
WARLEGGAN

I visited Warleggan (originally 'Worlegan', a name similar to a Welsh word meaning 'a high place') on a beautiful summer's afternoon of brilliant sunshine. Even so, there was a slightly eerie quality about this isolated village, situated in a pretty, tree-filled valley between the two large parishes of Cardinham and St Neot, about four miles due east of Bodmin. Yet it is not bleak, and the little church dedicated to St Bartholomew (not a local saint) nestles beneath tall beeches from which emanates the ceaseless cawing of rooks. Were it not for these trees, the church would be quite exposed for it stands nearly 800ft. above sea-level.

Struck by lightning in 1818, its steeple (one of few to be found in Cornwall) collapsed onto the building, causing a considerable amount of damage. It was never replaced, which accounts for the rather strange appearance of the tower onto which it was built. Of the three bells, two were sold in order to raise money for repairs, so that only one now survives.

The oldest part of the church is the nave which dates from the 11th century. The north wall is of rubble, for though ancient Cornish crosses had long been constructed of granite, the latter was not used for building purposes until the fifteenth century. The old cross outside the porch is thought to be eighth century and was for many years used as a gatepost. Adjacent to the church, a large house surrounded by trees was at one time the rectory.

Bounded by three rivers, the Dewy to the east, the Fowey to the south, and the charmingly named Bedalder on the west, Warleggan was once described in a guidebook as "the loneliest village on Bodmin Moor" – which indeed it was until not so long ago when the road was built connecting it with the A30 and the A38. The main centre is the nearby village of Mount, through which the mail coaches once travelled on what used to be the main road from Bodmin to Liskeard.

In common with other small Cornish parishes, Warleggan has in its time been rather neglected by some of its incumbents. Back in 1244, for instance, there was John Wak, the first recorded rector. He had many parishes and apparently lived in none of them. The second recorded was John Tremur, who absented himself from the parish from 1328 to 1331 whilst at Oxford. Being brilliantly clever, and also because the previous rector had let church and vicarage fall into disrepair, the Bishop gave him leave of absence.

Tremur's son, Ralph de Tremur, was also extremely clever. Instituted in 1331, he too had the Bishop's permission to study at Oxford. Extraordinary as it may sound, he never lived in the parish and never even went through it. After his resignation, he did visit it, however, on which occasion, believe it or not, he burgled the parsonage and set it on fire.

In 1706 came one, Daniel Baudris, who was a French refugee. He looked after the parish well and reported that there were twenty-six families in it and no dissenters. Samuel Gurney was rector in 1746, but he had two other churches, ran a grammar school, and lived a long way from the parish at Tregony. In 1774, there came a curate named Francis Cole, who was also vicar of Luxulyan. According to legend, he haunts the nearby road, and it is said that the wheels of his carriage are sometimes to be heard.

Yet the strangest of them all was an incumbent by the name of Frederick William Densham, who went to Warleggan in more recent times. Nothing was known about him when he first arrived in 1931; he was unpopular with the parishioners right from the start. As time went on, things grew worse and worse, his behaviour becoming ever more pathetic and bizarre. At one stage, he built an eighteen-foot wall around the rectory to keep his dogs in, neighbouring farmers having complained that they were worrying the sheep.

His parishioners found him domineering and his views outrageous.

Rough Tor, Bodmin Moor.

Soon folk started absenting themselves from church and ostracising it, so that after his death an entry was found in his service book which read, "No fog, no wind, no rain, no drizzle, no congregation". Another entry reported, "No congregation at any service". Ultimately the rector became so desperate that he wrote the names of former incumbents on pieces of card and propped them up in the pews, then preached to them and called them his congregation of ghosts. His end was sad, for in 1953 he collapsed and died suddenly on the staircase in the rectory, remaining there for two days until discovered by his parishioners. No trace at all of his incumbency remains in the church, and the rectory is now a private residence. "He was a rum customer!" said one elderly farmer.

The parish itself consists of isolated granite farms and houses, built to withstand the worst of the moorland weather. One hundred years ago its population was twice its present figure. The principal building was for many years a fine manor house known as Trengoffe Barton, which unfortunately was burnt down in recent times. Very large tin mines once existed in the area, and the Treveddoe mines and quarries were worked until 1945. Today it is dangerous to go near them.

In spite of the somewhat sinister atmosphere pervading it, I found the little village with its fifteenth-century church serene and peaceful. Even today it is not easy to locate. Yet it is worth seeking out, for, along with Jamaica Inn, Bolventor, Dozmary Pool, Brown Willy and Rough Tor, it constitutes yet another intriguing feature of the wild and bleak expanse known as Bodmin Moor.

32.
WESLEY IN CORNWALL

Close by an old tin-mine chimney with ruined engine house adjacent (one of many dotted around West Cornwall) is a deep circular hollow on the side of a hill with terraces cut into its grassy banks to form a huge amphitheatre. Situated near Redruth and once the centre of a great mining district, Gwennap Pit is the spot where John Wesley loved to preach, and the best-known of all his preaching places. Here the miners would gather each year in ever-growing numbers to hear the great preacher; and when, at close on seventy, he preached to a congregation of 32,000, he described it as "one of the most magnificent spectacles to be seen this side heaven".

John Wesley's connections with Cornwall are well-known, though the little cottage on Bodmin Moor which we found some years ago is probably less so. Located in the tiny hamlet of Trewint near the attractive village of Altarnun, a plaque on the cottage wall states that it was visited from time to time by Wesley. Only rediscovered and restored in the 1980s after years of neglect and decay, the cottage has since become a Methodist shrine.

Inside we found a leaflet which tells the story. One day in the year 1743 two strangers called at the cottage in Trewint, having travelled all the way from Bristol. Elizabeth Isbell, the owner, answered the door and invited them in; then she stoked up the fire, provided their horse with hay, and cooked a meal for them. She learnt from the two men that they were itinerant preachers, and before leaving they said they would return. When Elizabeth's husband, Digory, arrived back from work, she told him about the visitors.

On a stormy night many weeks later, as the Isbells were sitting in front of their fire, one of the two men, John Nelson, turned up again. Soaked to the skin, he was given a change of clothing, and later enter-

House at Altarnun with plaque, and steps used as pulpit by Wesley.

tained the couple with an account of his adventures since they had last met. He stayed the night, and by next morning news of his arrival had travelled throughout the district far and wide. Crowds began to gather, and John preached to them from the cottage porch.

This gave Digory, a craftsman by trade, the idea of building a spare room for the two men, one of whom was John Wesley. Every evening for the whole of that summer, after a hard day's work to support himself and his wife, he got busy with hammer and trowel. When the room was finished, Elizabeth put in it a bed, a table, a candlestick and a stool – just as the Shunamite woman in the Bible provided and fitted out a small chamber for the prophet Elisha – all ready for the preachers when they should return.

As well as John Wesley and Nelson, Watts, Doddridge and Downes also slept in the room, and whenever they came to the cottage, people would flock from all over the countryside to hear them. Some were hostile, and one day a wild mob came to the cottage door, cursing John Wesley and his friends, and threatening to exterminate them. Yet the good work which had been started had its effect on the life of the neighbourhood, and before long new chapels began to spring up and many people gathered Sunday by Sunday to worship in them.

Digory and Elizabeth died in 1795 and 1805 respectively, and their tomb may be seen in the churchyard at Altarnun. Their epitaph states that "they were the first who entertained the Methodist preachers in the country, and lived and died in that connection, but strictly adhered to the duties of the Established church."

Whilst at Oxford, John and Charles Wesley founded a club, the members of which pledged themselves to regular habits in Bible study and work. This was the beginning of the Methodist movement, which owes its origin to the two brothers. In Wesley's own words, they "resolved to live by rule and method", and it is from this saying that the title 'Methodist' is derived.

The Isbells' cottage at Trewint where Wesley stayed.

John Wesley, like his brother Charles, was of short stature, and he would often choose to stand on a rock or stone hedge when he preached, in order to make himself heard better. One of these rocks from which Wesley is said to have preached lies at the foot of Rosewall Hill near St Ives, and another has given the name of 'Wesley Rock' to a little village between Penzance and Madron. In Altarnun, too, may be seen, outside a house, a flight of steps used by Wesley as a pulpit.

It is thought that Gwennap Pit was originally a 'Plan-an-Guare' or place of the play, where Cornish miracle plays were performed. Held in earthen amphitheatres in the open fields, the country folk would flock from far and near to see them, camping around in tents and booths. The plays, which often lasted for three days, were described by an Elizabethan writer as a "kinde of Enterlude, compiled in Cornish out of some scripture history, with ... grossenes". Whatever 'grossness' existed, however, must later have been well and truly exorcised; for since Wesley's time, the name of Gwennap Pit has been known to Methodists throughout the world. Wesleyans still hold their Whit-Monday anniversary meetings there.

SOUTH-EAST CORNWALL
(including more recent memories)

33.
MEVAGISSEY

This picturesque village with its narrow streets and quaint shops is one of Cornwall's oldest fishing ports. Its name is derived from two saints, St Mewan and St Issey. In 1850, Mevagissey boasted eighty fishing vessels, an outer pier being built in 1866. At this time, the pilchard industry flourished, but to-day the old pilchard fleet has entirely disappeared. Though fishing is still carried on, it is on a greatly reduced scale.

A pre-war memory of Mevagissey is of sitting on the harbour wall with my sister, watching a water polo match.

The Harbour, Mevagissey.

34.
BOCONNOC

Up the valley of the River Lerryn, north of Lostwithiel, lies the little hamlet of Couch's Mill, nestling amongst woodland and still very much a part of old Cornwall. Also very much part of old Cornwall is the Boconnoc estate, lying eight miles from Liskeard and four from Lostwithiel. Bounded on the north by Braddock, on the south by St Veep, and on the west by St Winnow, it is said to have been a place of considerable note in the time of the Civil War; though it has apparently never been privileged with either fair or market.

Boconnoc is probably one of Cornwall's lesser-known historic homes, and is not easy to find unless you happen to know it is there. The white gate in Couch's Mill which leads to Boconnoc Church is kept locked during the week, only being opened ten minutes before morning service each Sunday; though there is access farther on towards Braddock.

Passing through this second gate, it is a surprise to find oneself in a magnificent deer park of some 140 acres; even more of a surprise, on driving along an avenue lined with blue hydrangeas just bursting into bloom (when we saw them), to behold a large grey mansion, with chapel and farm buildings standing adjacent.

Interestingly, Boconnoc is said to be one of the best examples of landscaping in Cornwall, though it was sad to see the house unlived in due to the need for extensive repairs, one end buttressed to support the sagging walls. In the 1970s there was talk of the building being pulled down, but extensive restoration is now being carried out. A gardener working on the estate obligingly opened up the chapel for us.

The volume *History of Cornwall* compiled by Fortescue Hitchins, gives information on 600 years or more of history at Boconnoc. Mentioned in the Domesday Book, it is included under 'Lands of the Count of Mortain in Cornwall', where it is referred to as 'Botchonod' (or

'Bochenod'). The pre-Conquest holder was Osferd (or Osfern), in whose time it comprised "two villeins, two beasts, twenty sheep, seven goats, 100 acres of woodland, and 40 acres of pasture". Worth 10/- yearly, its value had increased to 40/- by the time the Count received it.

Boconnoc is said to have been a residence to the most distinguished families in Cornwall. In the reign of Henry III (1216–1272), it appears to have belonged to the De Caucia family of St Minver, then to Sir Hugh Courtenay (killed at the Battle of Tewkesbury), continuing in the Courtenay family until forfeited to the Crown. At this time (mid-fifteenth century), 'Blekennoe House' as it was then called, was described as an "old turreted mansion".

In 1294, there appears to have been no church; though later on, in Wolsey's Inquisition of 1521, there is mention of a church with a small aisle and two larger aisles; also of "bells rung either with hand or foot", the bottom of the bells being not more than two feet from the floor.

After passing to the Crown, Boconnoc was granted to the Russell family, and in 1579 was sold by Francis, Earl of Bedford, to William Mohun, who erected the present house. On 4th August 1644, Sir Bernard Gascoine surprised and took possession of Boconnoc, at which time it was garrisoned by parliamentary forces under the command of the Earl of Essex. Five days afterwards, the King took up his lodging at the house, attempting, it is said, to corrupt the fidelity of Essex, and staying until 4th September when he retired to Liskeard. He returned in 1646, when he held his court at Boconnoc, on which occasion there was a warrant signed by him for "fishing in the Lerrin".

Boconnoc continued as the seat of the Mohun family until 1712, when the title became extinct, after which it came into the hands of the Pitt family. Thomas Pitt, Lord Camelford, re-modelled the house, adding a wing to the former structure, in which wing there was said to be a gallery 65ft. in length, which opened into a drawing-room and library. The gallery and several of the apartments were described as "ornamented with many elegant portraits, some dating from 1636". In the billiard room was

Boconnoc
estate.

the bust of Lord Camelford, and in the park were vestiges of some ancient lodemines, one of which had been worked in the reign of Charles I and again in the year 1750, though it was not sufficiently productive to defray the cost of the venture.

Boconnoc passed from the Pitt family to the Right Honourable Lord Grenville, who owned it until 1834. Around this time, the house was said to have had the appearance of "convenience rather than magnificence". The scenery is described as wooded with "retired vallies, and streams of a brook, the river Lerrin, which discharges itself into Fowey Harbour". Through these woods and "vallies", the late Lord Camelford had "carried a pleasant road about 6 miles in length, lined with beech and oak". It was stated that the "present owner (Lord Grenville) is only a transient visitor in Cornwall, and it is not to be expected that the house, gardens and grounds will hereafter be kept in that order by which the regular abode of a nobleman is generally distinguished." Mention is also made of the "elegant obelisk in the grounds, 123ft. high, standing on rising ground".

Coming more up-to-date, house and estate have been visited in recent years by the camera crew who filmed part of Winston Graham's *Poldark* series for television here.

35.
"... AND SHALL TRELAWNY DIE?"

Passing through the village of Pelynt (spelt 'Plint' in olden times and still pronounced 'Plint') lying four miles north-west of Looe, we stopped to look at the church, a well-kept little building containing much of interest, not least its connection with Bishop Trelawny. The Trelawny family, who could trace their roots back to Saxon times, lived at nearby Trelawne, an ancient house with a medieval chapel lying towards Looe. Jonathan Trelawny was born in 1650, and became an M.A. of Oxford University at the age of twenty-three. At thirty-five he was appointed Bishop of Bristol – an honour granted him in recognition of his military activities during Monmouth's rebellion.

Whilst at Bristol, Trelawny declined to read the Declaration of Indulgence throughout the diocese, and along with six others, was sent for trial. The famous poem connected with the event, which contains the well-known line, "And shall Trelawny die?", hangs on a wall of the south transept of the church, in what is known as the Trelawny aisle. All seven bishops were triumphantly acquitted, and in an attempt at conciliation, James II offered Trelawny the Bishopric of Exeter. With the arrival of William of Orange at Torbay, however, Trelawny welcomed the new King and took the Oath of Allegiance. William confirmed his appoint-ment to Exeter, and later he was promoted to Winchester, where he completed the building of the palace.

In the Trelawny aisle may also be seen the Bishop's Chair standing near to the family vault. The latter was discovered in 1833 and contained coffins covered with rich velvet, along with trophies which include hel-mets, gauntlets and escutcheons, as well as a large coffin bearing the inscription, "Sir Jonathan Trelawny, Bart. Right Reverend Father in God, Lord Bishop of Winchester ..."

The church is dedicated to St Nun (or Nonna), the mother of St

David of Wales, and was built or rebuilt by the Normans; although the present building, erected in the 1400s, contains no Norman remains. The Manor of Pelynt is mentioned in the Domesday Book, at which time it is thought possible that a small Celtic monastery existed there. In 1252, a house and garden was purchased at "Plenynt" by the Abbot of Newenham, it being taxed in 1283 by the Bishop of Exeter as the vicarage of "Plenent".

Also of interest is the Buller tomb of 1615, on which Francis Buller, High Sheriff of Cornwall in 1600, is shown with his wife, Thomasine, and their eight daughters and four sons. Also the engraving of William Achym carved in 1589, the year following the Armada, which depicts him in armour, breeches, ruff, sword, and dagger. The curiously crooked manner in which the face has been carved is said to denote that he died of a stroke.

Yet another Trelawny monument is considered to be one of the finest examples of a slate memorial anywhere in Cornwall. It is to Edward Trelawny (1630), and is also noteworthy for its inscription – "Here lies an honest lawyer, wot ye what, A thing for all the world to wonder at."

The parish of Pelynt contains an Iron Age camp, and in the Trelawny Valley at Ninnies, near Hobb's Park on the West Looe River may be seen the fascinating holy well known as St Nun* – though it is said to be difficult to find. A description of this well appears in Kelly's Directory of 1914. It is described as follows: "a small building with a gabled front, containing a rude, square-headed doorway about 4ft. high, leading into a kind of grotto with an arched roof. At the farther end of the floor is a round granite basin, carved on its exterior circumference with a series of Maltese Crosses enclosed in rings. Into this basin the water drips from an opening at the back, and escapes by a perforation at the bottom."

---

*The name Pelynt is a corruption of the Celtic Plu-nent, meaning the Parish of St Nonna.

36.
LOOE AND POLPERRO

These popular tourist attractions, though more crowded these days, are otherwise still as remembered except for, as everywhere else, the proliferation of arty-crafty and gift shops. A pre-war trip to Looe by coach included a memorable visit to the Rabbitry. Long since defunct, it was interesting, when in the town recently, to come upon the old building, which we only recognised by the plaque proclaiming its former use.

Mrs. Bray, author of a novel, *Trelawny of Trelawne*, which she wrote in 1830, describes Polperro at this time as having lost much but not all of its picturesqueness. Many of the old fishermen's cottages had been pulled down, their places taken by ugly modern houses.

"Looe", she went on to say, "beautiful as it is, is not to be compared with Polperro. The descent is so steep that I, not being accustomed to the path, could only get down by clinging to Mr. Bray's arm for support. It was slippery and so rocky that in some places there were steps cut in the road for the convenience of passengers. The view of the little port, the old town in the bottom, the cliffs, and the spiked rocks starting up in the wildest and most abrupt manner, breaking the direct sweep of the waves toward the harbour, altogether produce such a combination of magnificent coast scenery as may truly be called sublime."

Polperro, 1938.

Further back in time, in the reign of Henry VIII, Leland wrote about Polperro "... a smawle creke cawled *Paul Pier*, and a symple and poore village upon the est side of the same, of fisharmen, and the boates there fishing by (be) saved by a *Peere* or key."

THE ISLES OF SCILLY

37.
THE FORTUNATE ISLANDS

Situated way out in the Atlantic, twenty-eight miles off Land's End, the Isles of Scilly attract many visitors each year. It was not always thus, of course, and thirty years or so ago the islands seemed even more cut off than they do today. Not that they have become at all commercialised in recent years, for they are still as beautiful and unspoilt as ever they were. In fact, to make the crossing from Penzance in the *Scillonian* (or by helicopter) and land on St Mary's is to step back in time by about fifty years.

For the Scillies (or 'The Fortunate Islands', as the little archipelago used to be known) are today as Cornwall was before invaded by the motor-car. There is no pollution, and though a few more cars and buses are to be seen around Hugh Town these days, no rush, no bustle, and no mainland tensions. On every hand one is surrounded by incredibly white beaches beside translucent, unbelievably blue seas streaked with long, low miniature islets. Marram grass covers the sand-dunes, heather and ling predominate on higher exposed ground, while blue agapanthus is to be seen everywhere.

Inland it is a joy to traverse the network of peaceful country lanes

Picking narcissi, Scilly Isles, *c.*1900.

set amid a patchwork of little fields (or 'squares' as they are known). In these fields, with their high hedges (known as 'fences') to protect them against the winter gales, are grown the flowers for which Scilly is famous – narcissi, sweet-scented Soleil d'Or and daffodils. (The pittisporum hedges had to be replaced after being killed off during the gales of some years back.) The flowers are picked in close bud nowadays instead of in full bloom as in times past, to ensure that they arrive fresh at their mainland destinations – so one does not see many fields around the islands abloom with colour and Scilly Whites these days. Flowers exist everywhere though – in field, hedgerow and garden, and in March in particular there is a wide variety to be seen for the time of year.

In days gone by, the life of the islanders centred around the flower industry which was a thriving one. The months of November and December were particularly busy, and after the early picking in the fields, came the bunching and packing. Cottages everywhere threw open their doors, and ground-floor rooms became hives of industry and colour as folk young and old lent a hand. Later came the lifting and sorting of the bulbs ready for the next crop.

The western rocks with Bishop Rock Lighthouse in the background.

Sadly, the flower industry has seen a considerable decline in recent years, for it has become increasingly difficult for the islands, disadvantaged by distance, to compete with mainland markets. This cutback in their livelihood has been a source of great hardship to the islanders who have had to turn to the tourist industry as their main source of income. Flower exporting still continues, though on a smaller scale.

Trips by motor-launch to the off-islands, as they are called, are a particular attraction for the holidaymaker, and each morning during the season finds the quay at St Mary's filled with folk queuing up to board the boats. Yet the islands and their beaches never become crowded, and the Scilly boatmen – bearded, cheerful and weatherbeaten – are amongst the most reliable in the country, able to weave expertly between hidden sandbanks and rocks and to change course according to the state of the tide.

The never-static vista of islands and jagged outcrop can be confusing, and one learns with some surprise that every rock has a name. Intriguing ones, too, such as Crebawethan, Biggal of Gorregan, Crebinicks, Great Minalto, Mincarlo down towards the Bishop Rock; Hanjague, Menawethan, Great and Little Ganinick, Little Ganilly and Nornour in the Eastern Isles. The granite mass known as Men-o-Vaur resembles the western façade of a cathedral and – split into two right down the middle – it is a death-trap for anyone so foolish as to ignore the currents and the boatmen's warnings, and attempt to sail between the walls of sheer rock.

Trips to the Eastern Isles and the Western Rocks to see the seals and sea-birds are ever popular, though one can no longer witness the 'relief' of the Bishop Rock Lighthouse – that most westerly bastion of the British Isles. For having first been fitted with a helicopter pad, the lighthouse has now, along with others around the country, been mechanised. So the spectacle of the retiring lighthouse-keeper being winched aboard a motor-boat, or the mail being delivered, cannot now be enjoyed.

On all the islands, succulents and cacti abound in the hedges and flame trees blossom in June, along with yucca trees, palms, and huge Echium. For the bird-watcher, they are a paradise, with shag, cormorant, gull and petrel all nesting happily, particularly on the uninhabited islands such as Annet and Mincarlo, and puffin to be seen early in the season. Inland pools provide habitats for waterfowl, moorhen, coot, mallard and sedge warblers, as well as rarer species which turn up from time to time.

To stay on the off-islands is to step even farther back in time. Tresco, Bryher, St Martin's, St Agnes – each has its own personality, and most of us have our favourites. Tresco, the only island that is privately owned (by the Dorrien-Smith family) is world-famous for its exotic sub-tropical gardens containing specimens gathered from all corners of the Earth. If the appearance of hotels on Bryher and St Martin's seems a little incongruous, at least these buildings are low-lying and blend harmoniously with the landscape.

Most things on Scilly cannot change, however, and with its superb scenery, friendly islanders, leisurely lifestyle and fresh air blowing straight from the Atlantic, a holiday on the islands is an unforgettable experience and one to linger long in the memory.

38.
SOME SCILLY RELICS

For the archaeologically-minded, the Isles of Scilly possess a further interest – the many relics of the islands' dim and distant past which lie dotted around on every hand.

Bronze Age burial chambers are to be seen on the main island, and on many of the other islands and islets that comprise Scilly. One example of these ancient relics is to be found at Bants Carn lying on the north-west side of St Mary's, one-and-a-half miles from Hugh Town and close to the tiny hamlet called Telegraph. Roughly forty feet across, it follows the pattern of all such burial chambers, consisting of a massive stone slab (or capstone) resting on two uprights. The passage beneath extends some way back into the interior, and it would originally have been a chambered tomb used for collective burial during the Bronze Age (c.1900–800 B.C.). Of the type known as an 'entrance grave', it has long since been rifled of its contents; though there are on display in the island museum some excellent examples of funeral urns found in this and other similar tombs.

At Bants Carn, too, is a Romano-British village of two to three centuries A.D. on which work has been in progress for a number of years. This ancient settlement consists of eleven round or oval huts built of large, well-laid granite blocks, including a two-

Ancient burial chamber – St Mary's.

roomed house. Taken from this site and also to be seen in the museum is a unique collection of Roman coins and bronze brooches, as well as a display of different types of pottery covering the many years of the village's occupation. The museum also contains a Stone, Bronze and Iron Age collection of flints and stone tools, including Neolithic man-made objects – the earliest to be found on the islands.

Walking eastwards from Bants Carn round the northern tip of the island, one reaches Innisidgen, where two more tombs are to be found in close proximity to the cliff. Not the usual position for burial chambers, their siting is proof that the islands at one time extended much further outwards. A fourth tomb which is to be seen over on Porthellick Down in the south-east corner of the island. This one, approached by way of a well-kept grassy pathway, is the most imposing, being a perfect circle with a neatly grassed top, its shape somewhat reminiscent of a sponge-cake.

Visitors to Nor-Nour (one may land on some of the uninhabited islands, if one so wishes), will find yet another ancient settlement – this also being of Romano-Celtic origin. Here too are the remains of a habitation of Christian monks of the dark ages. Nor-Nour is just one of the 150 islands, islets and granite rocks that comprise Scilly.

Another and larger island is Samson, distinguishable by its twin hills, and the great curve of its white, shell-covered beach. It was Augustus Smith, the then governor of Scilly, who in the 1850s ordered the evacuation of this now uninhabited island. For the folk living there had become so poverty-stricken and unable to support themselves that they were reduced to feeding on limpets. The remains of some of their ruined cottages – and even empty limpet shells – are still to be seen on one of the twin hills, including that of 'Armorel', the heroine of the novel, *Armorel of Lyonesse*, by Sir Walter Besant, .

Another uninhabited island is St Helen's, conical-shaped and rising to a height of 144 feet. Here may be seen, buried in scrub, what remains of the rectangular walls of the oratory of St Elidius, the oldest Christian building of the islands. St Elidius arrived in Scilly during the Christian era and probably lived in the round hut on the west side of the site. A later church was built around the thirteenth century to accommodate the increasing number of pilgrims who came to visit the spot.

Amongst these was, it is said, the Viking, Olaf Trygvasson, later King of Norway, converted to Christianity here at the end of the tenth century. On this island, too, is to be seen a pest-house dating from 1756 where, in

Tresco Abbey.

olden times, unfortunate sufferers from the plague would be dropped off by passing ships to recuperate – or more likely to die.

Of the five inhabited islands, St Agnes (or Agnes, as it is familiarly known) lies at the most southerly point of the British Isles. With the tiny island of Gugh connected to it by a sand-bar on its eastern side, it possesses one of the loveliest beaches on Scilly – only dangerous for bathing when the tide is flowing over the bar. Gugh becomes an island at high-tide, when its two small houses are completely cut off.

Much of the downland on both Agnes and Gugh is of particular archaeological significance. On the far side of Gugh more burial chambers are to be found, whilst an ancient standing stone eight feet high is known as the 'Old Man of Gugh'. There is a curious pattern of pebbles on St Agnes known as the Troy Town Maze. Here too is the celebrated well of St Warna, a Celtic saint traditionally linked with wrecks. In years gone by, it is said, islanders would drop pins into the well, praying quaintly as they did so, "Good-night friends and foes, and God save us a ship before morning." This did not signify that they were wreckers, however, involved in the nefarious business of luring ships onto the rocks by night. In fact, there would have been no need for such action, because every rock in Scilly has been said to have claimed at least one victim. Even since 1700, 450 wrecks have been recorded on these treacherous shores.

On Tresco, an item of historical interest is twelfth-century St Nicholas Abbey, once occupied by monks from Tavistock – though not much remains nowadays except for the Norman Archway. Looking down the channel, with Bryher to the right and St Mary's and St Agnes in the distance, may be seen Cromwell's Castle, once possessing a battery of nine-pounders, and just above it, King Charles Castle which was never used. Tresco's church of St Nicholas, the patron saint of seafarers, was built in memory of Augustus Smith.

According to legend, the islands comprise the hilltops of the lost Arthurian land of Lyonesse, a view not supported by archaeologists. However, stone walls and other signs of landscape have been discovered on the sea-bed by divers, which seems to prove beyond doubt that the islands were once joined together in one great land mass. At low spring tides when the water is very shallow, it is possible to wade between some of the islands; though, as the tide turns very quickly, this could be a dangerous exercise and one not recommended to visitors, who should be wary unless having a boat in attendance. An amusing tale is told of an inhabitant of Tresco who decided he would like to go and live on Bryher. The tide being right, he pushed his belongings across the sand in a hand-cart.

An early meaning of the word 'silly' was fortunate (not 'foolish' as nowadays), which is why the islands have been equated with the Fortunate Isles of classical mythology. The story goes that the islanders got tired of jokes at their expense, so added the letter 'c'.

True or false, it is an amazing thought that this fantastic little archipelago has been separated from the mainland for at least the last 300,000 years. It is also remarkable that out of the 250 stone burial chambers which exist throughout England and Wales, eighty of them are to be found here on Scilly – three times as many as in the whole of Cornwall. Which only goes to show how important the islands must have been to Neolithic man.

INDEX

6291